THE MOTHER GOOSE
TREASURY

"No, no, my melodies will never die,
While nurses sing, or babies cry."
—Mother Goose, 1833

RAYMOND BRIGGS

THE MOTHER GOOSE TREASURY

A YEARLING BOOK

THE RHYMES ARE REPRODUCED
WITH ACKNOWLEDGEMENTS AND
GRATEFUL THANKS TO
PETER AND IONA OPIE

Published by
Dell Publishing Co., Inc.
1 Dag Hammarskjold Plaza
New York, New York 10017

The Rhymes are reproduced with acknowledgments and grateful
thanks to Peter and Iona Opie.

Copyright © 1966 by Raymond Briggs

Yearling ® TM 913705, Dell Publishing Co., Inc.

ISBN: 0-440-46408-0

Reprinted by arrangement with Coward, McCann Inc., a division of
the Putnam Publishing Group

Printed in the United States of America

One Previous Edition

December 1986

10 9 8 7 6 5 4 3 2 1

WAK

THE MOTHER GOOSE TREASURY
An index of first lines and familiar titles is at the back of the book

OLD MOTHER GOOSE AND
THE GOLDEN EGG

Old Mother Goose,
    When she wanted to wander,
Would ride through the air
    On a very fine gander.

Mother Goose had a house,
    'Twas built in a wood,
Where an owl at the door
    For sentinel stood.

She had a son Jack,
    A plain-looking lad,
He was not very good,
    Nor yet very bad.

She sent him to market,
    A live goose he bought;
See, mother, says he,
    I have not been for nought.

Jack's goose and her gander
    Grew very fond;
They'd both eat together,
    Or swim in the pond.

Jack found one fine morning,
    As I have been told,
His goose had laid him
    An egg of pure gold.

Jack ran to his mother
    The news for to tell,
She called him a good boy,
    And said it was well.

Jack sold his gold egg
   To a merchant untrue,
Who cheated him out of
   A half of his due.

Then Jack went a-courting
   A lady so gay,
As fair as the lily,
   And sweet as the May.

The merchant and squire
   Soon came at his back,
And began to belabour
   The sides of poor Jack.

Then old Mother Goose
   That instant came in,
And turned her son Jack
   Into famed Harlequin.

She then with her wand
　　Touched the lady so fine,
And turned her at once
　　Into sweet Columbine.

The gold egg in the sea
　　Was thrown away then,
When an odd fish brought her
　　The egg back again.

The merchant then vowed
　　The goose he would kill,
Resolving at once
　　His pockets to fill.

Jack's mother came in,
　　And caught the goose soon,
And mounting its back,
　　Flew up to the moon.

THREE MEN IN A TUB

Rub-a-dub-dub,
Three men in a tub,
And how do you think they got there?
The butcher, the baker,
The candlestick-maker,
They all jumped out of a rotten
potato,
'Twas enough to make a man stare.

PAT-A-CAKE

Pat-a-cake, pat-a-cake, baker's man,
Bake me a cake as fast as you can;
Pat it and prick it, and mark it with T,
Put it in the oven for Tommy and me.

7

OLD MOTHER HUBBARD AND HER DOG

    Old Mother Hubbard
    Went to the cupboard,
To fetch her poor dog a bone;
    But when she got there
    The cupboard was bare
And so the poor dog had none.

She went to the baker's
    To buy him some bread;
But when she came back
    The poor dog was dead.

She went to the undertaker's
    To buy him a coffin;
But when she came back
    The poor dog was laughing.

She took a clean dish
    To get him some tripe;
But when she came back
    He was smoking a pipe.

She went to the fishmonger's
    To buy him some fish;
But when she came back
    He was licking the dish.

She went to the tavern
    For white wine and red;
But when she came back
    The dog stood on his head.

She went to the fruiterer's
    To buy him some fruit;
But when she came back
    He was playing the flute.

She went to the tailor's
  To buy him a coat;
But when she came back
  He was riding a goat.

She went to the hatter's
  To buy him a hat;
But when she came back
  He was feeding the cat.

She went to the barber's
  To buy him a wig;
But when she came back
  He was dancing a jig.

She went to the cobbler's
  To buy him some shoes;
But when she came back
  He was reading the news.

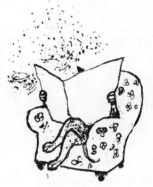

She went to the seamstress
  To buy him some linen;
But when she came back
  The dog was a-spinning.

She went to the hosier's
  To buy him some hose;
But when she came back
  He was dressed in his clothes.

The dame made a curtsey,
  The dog made a bow;
The dame said, Your servant,
  The dog said, Bow-wow.

THE LITTLE BOY
There was a little boy went into a barn,
   And lay down on some hay;
An owl came out and flew about,
   And the little boy ran away.

TO THE RAIN
Rain, rain, go away,
Come again another day,
Little Johnny wants to play.
Rain, rain, go to Spain,
Never show your face again.

YOU SHALL BE QUEEN
Lilies are white,
   Rosemary's green,
When I am king,
   You shall be queen.

10

BAA, BAA, BLACK SHEEP

Baa, baa, black sheep,
    Have you any wool?
Yes, sir, yes, sir,
    Three bags full;
One for the master,
    And one for the dame,
And one for the little boy
    Who lives down the lane.

HECTOR PROTECTOR

Hector Protector was dressed all in green;
Hector Protector was sent to the Queen.
The Queen did not like him,
No more did the King;
So Hector Protector was sent back again.

THE LITTLE MAN

There was a little man, and he had a little gun,
   And his bullets were made of lead, lead, lead;
He went to the brook, and shot a little duck,
   Right through the middle of the head, head, head.
He carried it home to his old wife Joan,
   And bade her a fire for to make, make, make,
To roast the little duck he had shot in the brook,
   And he'd go and fetch her the drake, drake, drake

THE CROOKED MAN

There was a crooked man,
   And he walked a crooked mile,
He found a crooked sixpence
   Against a crooked stile;
He bought a crooked cat,
   Which caught a crooked mouse,
And they all lived together
   In a little crooked house.

THE OLD WOMAN'S THREE COWS

There was an old woman had three cows,
   Rosy and Colin and Dun.
Rosy and Colin were sold at the fair,
And Dun broke her heart in a fit of despair,
So there was an end of her three cows,
   Rosy and Colin and Dun.

IPSEY WIPSEY

Ipsey Wipsey spider
   Climbing up the spout;
Down came the rain
   And washed the spider out;
Out came the sunshine
   And dried up all the rain;
Ipsey Wipsey spider
   Climbing up again.

BEDTIME

Come, let's to bed,
Says Sleepy-head;
Tarry a while, says Slow;
Put on the pot,
Says Greedy-gut,
We'll sup before we go.

THE PIE

Who made the pie?
I did.
Who stole the pie?
He did.
Who found the pie?
She did.
Who ate the pie?
You did.
Who cried for pie?
We all did.

TOMMY AND BESSY

As Tommy Snooks and Bessy Brooks
Were walking out one Sunday,
Says Tommy Snooks to Bessy Brooks,
Tomorrow will be Monday.

JACK SPRAT

Jack Sprat could eat no fat,
His wife could eat no lean,
And so between them both, you see,
They licked the platter clean.

A GIRL IN THE ARMY

A girl in the army
She longed for a baby,
She took her father's greyhound
And laid it in the cradle.
Lullaby, Baby Bow Wow,
Long legs hast thou,
And wasn't it for thy cold snout
I would kiss thee now, now.

BOY BLUE

Little Boy Blue,
  Come blow your horn,
The sheep's in the meadow,
  The cow's in the corn.
Where is the boy
  Who looks after the sheep?
He's under a haystack
  Fast asleep.
Will you wake him?
  No, not I,
For if I do,
  He's sure to cry.

MON	TUE	WED	THUR	FRI	SAT	SUN

A WEEK OF BIRTHDAYS

Monday's child is fair of face,
Tuesday's child is full of grace,
Wednesday's child is full of woe,
Thursday's child has far to go,
Friday's child is loving and giving,
Saturday's child works hard for its
    living,
But the child that's born on the
    Sabbath day
Is bonny and blithe, and good and
    gay.

DICKY DILVER

Little Dicky Dilver
Had a wife of silver;
He took a stick and broke her back
And sold her to the miller;
The miller wouldn't have her
So he threw her in the river.

TOM TINKER'S DOG

Bow, wow, wow,
Whose dog art thou?
Little Tom Tinker's dog,
Bow, wow, wow.

WILLIE WINKIE

Wee Willie Winkie runs through the town,
Upstairs and downstairs in his night-gown,
Rapping at the window, crying through the lock,
Are the children all in bed, for now it's eight o'clock?

TO THE SNOW

Snow, snow faster,
Ally-ally-blaster;
The old woman's plucking her geese,
Selling the feathers a penny a piece.

THE DOVE SAYS

The dove says, Coo, coo,
What shall I do?
I can scarce maintain two.
Pooh, pooh, says the wren,
I have ten,
And keep them all like gentlemen.
Curr dhoo, curr dhoo,
Love me, and I'll love you.

MOTHER SHUTTLE

Old Mother Shuttle,
    Lived in a coal-scuttle
Along with her dog and her cat;
    What they ate I can't tell,
    But 'tis known very well
That not one of the party was fat.

    Old Mother Shuttle
    Scoured out her coal-scuttle,
And washed both her dog and her cat;
    The cat scratched her nose,
    So they came to hard blows,
And who was the gainer by that?

MY MAMMY'S MAID

Dingty diddlety,
    My mammy's maid,
She stole oranges,
    I am afraid;
Some in her pocket,
    Some in her sleeve,
She stole oranges,
    I do believe.

SING A SONG OF SIXPENCE

Sing a song of sixpence,
  A pocket full of rye;
Four and twenty blackbirds,
  Baked in a pie.

When the pie was opened,
  The birds began to sing;
Was not that a dainty dish,
  To set before a king?

The king was in his counting-house,
  Counting out his money;
The queen was in the parlour
  Eating bread and honey.

The maid was in the garden,
  Hanging out the clothes,
When down came a blackbird
  And pecked off her nose.

RAIN BEFORE SEVEN

Rain before seven,
Fine before eleven.

TO THE CUCKOO
Cuckoo, cuckoo, what do you do?
In April I open my bill;
In May I sing all day;
In June I change my tune;
In July away I fly;
In August away I must.

THE NORTH WIND
The north wind doth blow,
And we shall have snow,
And what will poor Robin do then,
  Poor thing?
He'll sit in a barn,
And keep himself warm,
And hide his head under his wing,
  Poor thing.

JEREMIAH OBADIAH
Jeremiah Obadiah, puff, puff, puff.
When he gives his messages he snuffs, snuffs, snuffs,
When he goes to school by day, he roars, roars, roars,
When he goes to bed at night he snores, snores, snores,
When he goes to Christmas treat he eats plum-duff,
Jeremiah Obadiah, puff, puff, puff.

GRIG'S PIG
Grandfa' Grig
Had a pig,
In a field of clover;
Piggy died,
Granfa' cried,
And all the fun was over.

GOOSEY GANDER

Goosey, goosey gander,
   Wither shall I wander?
Upstairs and downstairs
   And in my lady's chamber.
There I met an old man
   Who would not say his prayers,
I took him by the left leg
   And threw him down the stairs.

JUMPING JOAN

Here am I,
   Little Jumping Joan;
When nobody's with me
   I'm all alone.

THE DONKEY

If I had a donkey that wouldn't go,
Would I beat him? Oh no, no.
I'd put him in the barn and give him some corn.
The best little donkey that ever was born.

21

TOM

Tom, Tom, the piper's son,
Stole a pig and away he run;
 The pig was eat,
 And Tom was beat,
And Tom went howling down the street.

HOW TO SLEEP EASY
To sleep easy all night,
Let your supper be light,
Or else you'll complain
Of a stomach in pain.

Roses are red,
 Violets are blue,
Sugar is sweet
 And so are you.

MAN OF DERBY

A little old man of Derby,
How do you think he served me?
He took away my bread and cheese,
And that is how he served me.

TAILOR OF BICESTER

The tailor of Bicester,
  He has but one eye;
He cannot cut a pair of green
    galligaskins,
  If he were to die.

THE MAN IN THE MOON

The man in the moon drinks claret,
But he is a dull jack-a-dandy;
Would he know a sheep's head from
    a carrot,
He should learn to drink cider and
    brandy.

23

THREE CHILDREN SLIDING

Three children sliding on the ice,
  Upon a summer's day,
As it fell out, they all fell in,
  The rest they ran away.

Now had these children been at home,
  Or sliding on dry ground,
Ten thousand pounds to one penny
  They had not all been drowned.

You parents all that children have,
  And you that have got none,
If you would have them safe abroad,
  Pray keep them safe at home.

THE STAR

Twinkle, twinkle, little star,
How I wonder what you are!
Up above the world so high,
Like a diamond in the sky.

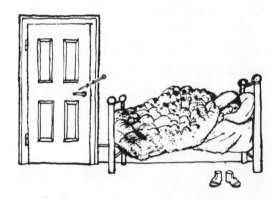

A LITTLE MAID

There was a little maid, and she was afraid
That her sweetheart would come unto her;
So she went to bed, and covered up her head,
And fastened the door with a skewer.

A RAT

There was a rat, for want of stairs,
Went down a rope to say his prayers.

THE BRAVE
OLD DUKE OF YORK

Oh, the brave old Duke of York,
 He had ten thousand men;
He marched them up to the top of the hill,
 And he marched them down again.
And when they were up, they were up,
 And when they were down, they were down,
And when they were only half way up,
 They were neither up nor down.

CHARLIE WARLIE

Charlie Warlie had a cow,
Black and white about the brow;
Open the gate and let her through,
Charlie Warlie's old cow.

THE GIANT

Fee, fi, fo, fum,
I smell the blood of an Englishman:
Be he alive or be he dead,
I'll grind his bones to make my bread.

CORPORAL BULL

Here's Corporal Bull
A strong hearty fellow,
Who not used to fighting
Set up a loud bellow.

RICHES

My father died a month ago
  And left me all his riches;
A feather bed, a wooden leg,
  And a pair of leather breeches;
A coffee pot without a spout,
  A cup without a handle,
A tobacco pipe without a lid,
  And half a farthing candle.

Matthew, Mark, Luke, and John,
Hold my horse till I leap on,
Hold him steady, hold him sure,
And I'll get over the misty moor.

SEE-SAW
See-saw, Margery Daw,
Jacky shall have a new master;
Jacky shall have but a penny a day,
Because he can't work any faster.

THE KILKENNY CATS
There were once two cats of Kilkenny.
Each thought there was one cat too many;
So they fought and they fit,
And they scratched and they bit,
   Till, excepting their nails,
   And the tips of their tails,
Instead of two cats, there weren't any.

See-saw, Margery Daw,
Sold her bed and lay upon straw;
Was not she a dirty slut
To sell her bed and lie in the dirt.

28

ROBIN AND JENNY

Jenny Wren fell sick
   Upon a merry time,
In came Robin Redbreast
   And brought her sops and wine.
Eat well of the sop, Jenny,
   Drink well of the wine,
Thank you, Robin, kindly,
   You shall be mine.
Jenny Wren got well,
   And stood upon her feet;
And told Robin plainly,
   She loved him not a bit.
Robin he got angry,
   And hopped upon a twig,
Saying, Out upon you, fie upon you,
   Bold faced jig!

KING OF THE CASTLE

I'm the king of the castle,
Get down you dirty rascal.

MY LITTLE DOG

Oh where, oh where has my little dog gone?
   Oh where, oh where can he be?
With his ears cut short and his tail cut long,
   Oh where, oh where is he?

JERRY HALL

Jerry Hall,
He is so small,
A rat could eat him,
Hat and all.

THE HOUSE THAT JACK BUILT

This is the house
that Jack built.

This is the malt
That lay in the house
that Jack built.

This is the rat,
That ate the malt
That lay in the house
that Jack built.

This is the cat,
That killed the rat,
That ate the malt
That lay in the house
 that Jack built.

This is the dog,
That worried the cat,
That killed the rat,
That ate the malt
That lay in the house
 that Jack built.

This is the cow with the crumpled horn,
That tossed the dog,
That worried the cat,
That killed the rat,
That ate the malt
That lay in the house
 that Jack built.

This is the maiden all forlorn,
That milked the cow with the crumpled horn,
That tossed the dog,
That worried the cat,
That killed the rat,
That ate the malt
That lay in the house
 that Jack built.

This is the man all tattered and torn,
That kissed the maiden all forlorn,
That milked the cow with the crumpled horn,
That tossed the dog,
That worried the cat,
That killed the rat,
That ate the malt
That lay in the house
    that Jack built.

This is the priest all shaven and shorn,
That married the man all tattered and torn,
That kissed the maiden all forlorn,
That milked the cow with the crumpled horn,
That tossed the dog,
That worried the cat,
That killed the rat,
That ate the malt
That lay in the house
    that Jack built.

This is the cock that crowed in the morn,
That waked the priest all shaven and shorn,
That married the man all tattered and torn,
That kissed the maiden all forlorn,
That milked the cow with the crumpled horn,
That tossed the dog,
That worried the cat,
That killed the rat,
That ate the malt
That lay in the house
    that Jack built.

This is the farmer sowing his corn,
That kept the cock that crowed in the morn,
That waked the priest all shaven and shorn,
That married the man all tattered and torn,
That kissed the maiden all forlorn,
That milked the cow with the crumpled horn,
That tossed the dog,
That worried the cat,
That killed the rat,
That ate the malt
That lay in the house
　　that Jack built.

This is the horse and the hound and the horn,
That belonged to the farmer sowing his corn,
That kept the cock that crowed in the morn,
That waked the priest all shaven and shorn,
That married the man all tattered and torn,
That kissed the maiden all forlorn,
That milked the cow with the crumpled horn,
That tossed the dog,
That worried the cat,
That killed the rat,
That ate the malt
That lay in the house
　　that Jack built.

SIMPLE SIMON

Simple Simon met a pieman
   Going to the fair;
Says Simple Simon to the pieman,
   Let me taste your ware.

Says the pieman to Simple Simon,
   Show me first your penny;
Says Simple Simon to the pieman,
   Indeed I have not any.

Simple Simon went a-fishing,
   For to catch a whale;
All the water he had got
   Was in his mother's pail.

Simple Simon went a-hunting,
   For to catch a hare;
He rode a goat about the streets,
   But couldn't find one there.

He went to catch a dickey bird,
   And thought he could not fail,
Because he'd got a little salt,
   To put upon its tail.

He went to shoot a wild duck,
    But wild duck flew away;
Says Simon, I can't hit him,
    Because he will not stay.

He went to ride a spotted cow,
    That had a little calf;
She threw him down upon the ground,
    Which made the people laugh.

Once Simon made a great snowball,
    And brought it in to roast;
He laid it down before the fire,
    And soon the ball was lost.

He went to try if cherries ripe
    Did grow upon a thistle;
He pricked his finger very much
    Which made poor Simon whistle.

He went for water in a sieve,
    But soon it all ran through;
And now poor Simple Simon
    Bids you all adieu.

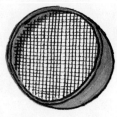

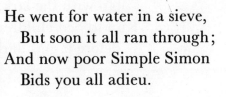

MAN OF THESSALY

There was a man of Thessaly
    And he was wondrous wise,
He jumped into a bramble bush
    And scratched out both his eyes.
And when he saw his eyes were out,
    With all his might and main
He jumped into another bush
    And scratched them in again.

DOCTOR FOSTER

Old Doctor Foster
Went to Gloucester
To preach the word of God;
    When he came there,
    He sat in a chair,
And gave all the people a nod.

DIDDLE, DIDDLE, DUMPLING

Diddle, diddle, dumpling, my son John,
Went to bed with his trousers on;
One shoe off, and one shoe on,
Diddle, diddle, dumpling, my son John.

BEDTIME

Down with the lambs
    Up with the lark,
Run to bed children
    Before it gets dark.

A STRANGE PIG

As I went to Bonner,
 I met a pig
 Without a wig,
Upon my word and honour.

CAUTION

Mother, may I go out to swim?
 Yes, my darling daughter.
Hang your clothes on a hickory limb
 And don't go near the water.

THE BRAVE PRIEST

The little priest of Felton,
The little priest of Felton,
He killed a mouse within his house,
And nobody there to help him.

SHORT SONG

There was an old crow
 Sat upon a clod;
That's the end of my song.
 —That's odd.

JACK
Jack be nimble,
  Jack be quick,
Jack jump over
  The candlestick.

38

BED
Go to bed first,
A golden purse;
Go to bed second,
A golden pheasant;
Go to bed third,
A golden bird.

THREE A-BED
He that lies at the stock,
Shall have a gold rock;
He that lies at the wall,
Shall have a gold ball;
He that lies in the middle,
Shall have a gold fiddle.

ONE, TWO

1, 2,
Buckle my shoe;

3, 4,
Knock at the door;

5, 6,
Pick up sticks;

7, 8,
Lay them straight;

9, 10,
A big fat hen;

11, 12,
Dig and delve;

13, 14,
Maids a-courting;

15, 16,
Maids in the kitchen;

17, 18,
Maids in waiting;

19, 20,
My plate's empty.

UNDER A HILL

There was an old woman
Lived under a hill,
And if she's not gone
She lives there still.

LITTLE MOPPET

I had a little moppet,
I kept it in my pocket
And fed it on corn and hay;
There came a proud beggar
And said he would wed her,
And stole my little moppet away.

PUNCH AND JUDY

Punch and Judy
   Fought for a pie;
Punch gave Judy
   A knock in the eye.
Says Punch to Judy,
   Will you have any more?
Says Judy to Punch,
   My eye is too sore.

DOCTOR FOSTER

Doctor Foster went to Gloucester
In a shower of rain;
He stepped in a puddle,
Right up to his middle,
And never went there again.

THE WREN HUNT

We will go to the wood, says Robin to Bobbin,
We will go to the wood, says Richard to Robin.
We will go to the wood, says John all alone,
We will go to the wood, says everyone.

What to do there? says Robin to Bobbin,
What to do there? says Richard to Robin,
What to do there? says John all alone,
What to do there? says everyone.

We'll shoot at a wren, says Robin to Bobbin,
We'll shoot at a wren, says Richard to Robin,
We'll shoot at a wren, says John all alone,
We'll shoot at a wren, says everyone.

She's down, she's down, says Robin to Bobbin,
She's down, she's down, says Richard to Robin,
 She's down, she's down, says John all alone,
She's down, she's down, says everyone.

She is dead, she is dead, says Robin to Bobbin,
She is dead, she is dead, says Richard to Robin.
She is dead, she is dead, says John all alone,
She is dead, she is dead, says everyone.

Then pounce, then pounce, says Robin to Bobbin,
Then pounce, then pounce, says Richard to Robin,
Then pounce, then pounce, says John all alone,
Then pounce, then pounce, says everyone.

44

How get her home? says Robin to Bobbin,
How get her home? says Richard to Robin,
How get her home? says John all alone,
How get her home? says everyone.

In a cart with six horses, says Robin to Bobbin,
In a cart with six horses, says Richard to Robin,
In a cart with six horses, says John all alone,
In a cart with six horses, says everyone.

Then hoist, boys, hoist, says Robin to Bobbin,
Then hoist, boys, hoist, says Richard to Robin,
Then hoist, boys, hoist, says John all alone,
Then hoist, boys, hoist, says everyone.

How shall we dress her? says Robin to Bobbin,
How shall we dress her? says Richard to Robin,
How shall we dress her? says John all alone,
How shall we dress her? says everyone.

We'll hire seven cooks, says Robin to Bobbin,
We'll hire seven cooks, says Richard to Robin,
We'll hire seven cooks, says John all alone,
We'll hire seven cooks, says everyone.

How shall we boil her? says Robin to Bobbin,
How shall we boil her? says Richard to Robin,
How shall we boil her? says John all alone,
How shall we boil her? says everyone.

In the brewer's big pan, says Robin to Bobbin,
In the brewer's big pan, says Richard to Robin,
In the brewer's big pan, says John all alone,
In the brewer's big pan, says everyone.

JACK AND JILL
AND
OLD DAME DOB

Jack and Jill
Went up the hill,
To fetch a pail of water;
Jack fell down,
And broke his crown,
And Jill came tumbling after.

Then up Jack got,
And home did trot,
As fast as he could caper;
To old Dame Dob,
Who patched his nob
With vinegar and brown paper.

When Jill came in,
How she did grin
To see Jack's paper plaster;
Her mother, vexed,
Did whip her next,
For laughing at Jack's disaster.

Now Jack did laugh
And Jill did cry,
But her tears did soon abate;
Then Jill did say,
That they should play
At see-saw across the gate.

COCK-CROW

The cock's on the wood pile
　　Blowing his horn,
The bull's in the barn
　　A-threshing the corn,
The maids in the meadow
　　Are making the hay,
The ducks in the river
　　Are swimming away.

GENERAL MONK

Little General Monk
Sat upon a trunk,
Eating a crust of bread;
There fell a hot coal
And burnt in his clothes a hole,
Now little General Monk is dead.

THE DUNCE

Ring the bells, ring!
Hip, hurrah for the King!
The dunce fell into the pool, oh!
The dunce was going to school, oh!
The groom and the cook
Fished him out with a hook,
And he piped his eye like a fool, oh!

TO THE SNAIL

Snail, snail, put out your horns,
And I'll give you bread and barley corns.

MILKING

Cushy cow, bonny, let down thy milk,
And I will give thee a gown of silk;
A gown of silk and a silver tee,
If thou wilt let down thy milk for me.

GOING TO BED

Go to bed late,
Stay very small;
Go to bed early,
Grow very tall.

THE TWELVE DAYS OF CHRISTMAS

The first day of Christmas
My true love sent to me
A partridge in a pear tree.

The second day of Christmas
My true love sent to me
Two turtle doves, and
A partridge in a pear tree.

The third day of Christmas
My true love sent to me
Three French hens,
Two turtle doves, and
A partridge in a pear tree.

The fourth day of Christmas
My true love sent to me
Four colly birds,
Three French hens,
Two turtle doves, and
A partridge in a pear tree.

The fifth day of Christmas
My true love sent to me
Five gold rings,
Four colly birds,
Three French hens,
Two turtle doves, and
A partridge in a pear tree.

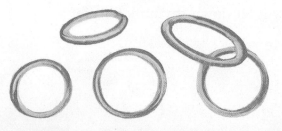

The sixth day of Christmas
My true love sent to me
Six geese a-laying,
Five gold rings,
Four colly birds,
Three French hens,
Two turtle doves, and
A partridge in a pear tree.

The seventh day of Christmas
My true love sent to me
Seven swans a-swimming,
Six geese a-laying,
Five gold rings,
Four colly birds,
Three French hens,
Two turtle doves, and
A partridge in a pear tree.

The eighth day of Christmas
My true love sent to me
Eight maids a-milking,
Seven swans a-swimming,
Six geese a-laying,
Five gold rings,
Four colly birds,
Three French hens,
Two turtle doves, and
A partridge in a pear tree.

The ninth day of Christmas
My true love sent to me
Nine drummers drumming,
Eight maids a-milking,
Seven swans a-swimming,
Six geese a-laying,
Five gold rings,
Four colly birds,
Three French hens,
Two turtle doves, and
A partridge in a pear tree.

51

The tenth day of Christmas
My true love sent to me
Ten pipers piping,
Nine drummers drumming,
Eight maids a-milking,
Seven swans a-swimming,
Six geese a-laying,
Five gold rings,
Four colly birds,
Three French hens,
Two turtle doves, and
A partridge in a pear tree.

The eleventh day of Christmas
My true love sent to me
Eleven ladies dancing,
Ten pipers piping,
Nine drummers drumming,
Eight maids a-milking,
Seven swans a-swimming,
Six geese a-laying,
Five gold rings,
Four colly birds,
Three French hens,
Two turtle doves, and
A partridge in a pear tree.

The twelfth day of Christmas
My true love sent to me
Twelve lords a-leaping,
Eleven ladies dancing,
Ten pipers piping,
Nine drummers drumming,
Eight maids a-milking,
Seven swans a-swimming,
Six geese a-laying,
Five gold rings,
Four colly birds,
Three French hens,
Two turtle doves, and
A partridge in a pear tree.

TAFFY WAS A WELSHMAN

Taffy was a Welshman,
   Taffy was a thief,
Taffy came to my house
   And stole a piece of beef.

I went to Taffy's house,
   Taffy wasn't in,
I jumped upon his Sunday hat
   And poked it with a pin.

Taffy was a Welshman,
   Taffy was a sham,
Taffy came to my house
   And stole a leg of lamb.

I went to Taffy's house,
   Taffy was not there,
I hung his coat and trousers
   To roast before a fire.

Taffy was a Welshman,
   Taffy was a cheat,
Taffy came to my house
   And stole a piece of meat.

I went to Taffy's house,
   Taffy wasn't home;
Taffy came to my house
   And stole a marrow bone.

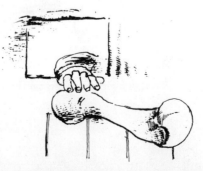

TWO PIG STORIES

This little pig went to market,
This little pig stayed at home,
This little pig had roast beef,
This little pig had none,
And this little pig cried, Wee-wee-
      wee-wee-wee,
  I can't find my way home.

This little pig had a rub-a-dub,
This little pig had a scrub-a-scrub,
This little pig-a-wig ran upstairs,
This little pig-a-wig called out, Bears!
Down came the jar with a loud
    Slam! Slam!
And this little pig had all the jam.

THE STORY OF THE LITTLE WOMAN

There was a little woman,
  As I have heard tell,
She went to market
  Her eggs for to sell,
She went to market
  All on a market day,
And she fell asleep
  On the King's highway.

There came by a pedlar
  His name was Stout,
He cut her petticoats
  All round about;
He cut her petticoats
  Up to her knees,
Which made the poor woman
  To shiver and sneeze.

When the little woman
  Began to awake,
She began to shiver,
  And she began to shake;
She began to shake,
  And she began to cry,
Goodness mercy on me,
  This is none of I!

If it be not I,
  As I suppose it be,
I have a little dog at home,
  And he knows me;
If it be I,
  He'll wag his little tail,
And if it be not I,
  He'll loudly bark and wail.

56

Home went the little woman,
  All in the dark,
Up jumped the little dog,
  And he began to bark.
He began to bark,
  And she began to cry,
Goodness mercy on me,
  I see I be not I!

This poor little woman
  Passed the night on a stile,
She shivered with cold,
  And she trembled the while;
She slept not a wink
  But was all night awake,
And was heartily glad
  When morning did break.

There came by the pedlar
  Returning from town,
She asked him for something
  To match her short gown,
The sly pedlar rogue
  Showed the piece he'd purloined,
Said he to the woman,
  It will do nicely joined.

She pinned on the piece,
  And exclaimed, What a match!
I am lucky indeed
  Such a bargain to catch.
The dog wagged his tail,
  And she began to cry,
Goodness mercy on me,
  I've discovered it be I!

HUSH-A-BYE

Hush-a-bye, baby, on the tree top,
When the wind blows the cradle will rock;
When the bough breaks the cradle will fall,
Down will come baby, cradle, and all.

58

BOYS AND GIRLS

What are little boys made of, made of?
What are little boys made of?
    Frogs and snails
    And puppy-dogs' tails,
That's what little boys are made of.

What are little girls made of, made of?
What are little girls made of?
    Sugar and spice
    And all things nice,
That's what little girls are made of.

THE DEATH AND BURIAL
OF COCK ROBIN

Who killed Cock Robin?
 I, said the Sparrow,
 With my bow and arrow,
I killed Cock Robin.

Who saw him die?
 I, said the Fly,
 With my little eye,
I saw him die.

Who caught his blood?
 I, said the Fish,
 With my little dish,
I caught his blood.

Who'll make his shroud?
 I said the Beetle,
 With my thread and needle,
I'll make the shroud.

Who'll dig his grave?
 I, said the Owl,
 With my pick and shovel,
I'll dig his grave.

Who'll be the parson?
 I, said the Rook,
 With my little book,
I'll be the parson.

Who'll be the clerk?
 I, said the Lark,
 If it's not in the dark,
I'll be the clerk.

Who'll carry the link?
 I, said the Linnet,
 I'll fetch it in a minute,
I'll carry the link.

Who'll be chief mourner?
 I, said the Dove,
 I mourn for my love,
I'll be chief mourner.

Who'll carry the coffin?
 I, said the Kite,
 If it's not through the night,
I'll carry the coffin.

Who'll bear the pall?
 We, said the Wren,
 Both the cock and the hen,
We'll bear the pall.

Who'll sing a psalm?
 I, said the Thrush,
 As she sat on a bush,
I'll sing a psalm.

Who'll toll the bell?
 I, said the Bull,
 Because I can pull,
So Cock Robin, farewell.

All the birds of the air
 Fell a-sighing and a-sobbing,
When they heard the bell toll
 For poor Cock Robin.

LITTLE MISS MUFFET

Little Miss Muffet
Sat on a tuffet,
Eating her curds and whey;
There came a big spider,
Who sat down beside her
And frightened Miss Muffet away.

THE LITTLE BOY

Little boy, little boy, where were you born?
Up in the Highlands among the green corn.
Little boy, little boy, where did you sleep?
In the byre with the kye, in the cot with the sheep.

JOLLY RED NOSE

Nose, nose,
   Jolly red nose,
And what gave thee
   That jolly red nose?
Nutmeg and ginger,
   Cinnamon and cloves,
That's what gave me
   This jolly red nose.

GREGORY GRIGGS

Gregory Griggs, Gregory Griggs,
Had twenty-seven different wigs.
He wore them up, he wore them
   down,
To please the people of the town;
He wore them east, he wore them
   west,
But he never could tell which he
   loved the best.

63

THE MAD FAMILY

There was a mad man he had a mad wife,
And they lived in a mad town;
And they had children three at birth,
  And mad they were every one.
The father was mad, the mother was mad,
  And the children mad beside;
And they all got on a mad horse,
  And madly they did ride.
They rode by night and they rode by day,
  Yet never a one of them fell;
They rode so madly all the way,
  Till they came to the gates of hell.
Old Nick was glad to see them so mad,
  And gladly let them in:
But he soon grew sorry to see them so merry
And let them out again.

LITTLE NAG

I had a little nag
    That trotted up and down;
I bridled him, and saddled him,
    And trotted out of town.

TWEEDLEDUM AND TWEEDLEDEE

Tweedledum and Tweedledee
    Agreed to have a battle,
For Tweedledum said Tweedledee
    Had spoiled his nice new rattle.
Just then flew by a monstrous crow
    As black as a tar-barrel,
Which frightened both the heroes so,
    They quite forgot their quarrel.

66

POLL PARROT

Little Poll Parrot
Sat in his garret
Eating toast and tea;
A little brown mouse
Jumped into the house
And stole it all away.

THE FLYING PIG

Dickery, dickery, dare,
The pig flew up in the air;
The man in brown
Soon brought him down,
Dickery, dickery, dare.

THE STORY OF THE OLD WOMAN AND HER PIG

An old woman went to market and bought a pig;
Pig had four legs,
But pig would not go.
Well, says the old woman, what shall I do?

She went a little farther and she calls to a dog,
Dog, dog, bite pig,
Pig will not go,
And I should have been at home two hours ago.
  But the dog would not.

She went a little farther and she calls to a stick,
Stick, stick, beat dog,
Dog won't bite pig,
Pig will not go,
And I should have been at home two hours ago.
  But the stick would not.

She went a little farther and she calls to a fire,
Fire, fire, burn stick,
Stick won't beat dog,
Dog won't bite pig,
Pig will not go,
And I should have been at home two hours ago.
  But the fire would not.

68

She went a little farther and she calls to some water,
Water, water, quench fire,
Fire won't burn stick,
Stick won't beat dog,
Dog won't bite pig,
Pig will not go,
And I should have been at home two hours ago.
    But the water would not.

She went a little farther and she calls to an ox,
Ox, ox, drink water,
Water won't quench fire,
Fire won't burn stick,
Stick won't beat dog,
Dog won't bite pig,
Pig will not go,
And I should have been at home two hours ago.
But the ox would not.

She went a little farther and she calls to a butcher,
Butcher, butcher, kill ox,
Ox won't drink water,
Water won't quench fire,
Fire won't burn stick,
Stick won't beat dog,
Dog won't bite pig,
Pig will not go,
And I should have been at home two hours ago.
    But the butcher would not.

She went a little farther and she calls to a rope,
Rope, rope, hang butcher,
Butcher won't kill ox,
Ox won't drink water,
Water won't quench fire,
Fire won't burn stick,
Stick won't beat dog,
Dog won't bite pig,
Pig will not go,
And I should have been at home two hours ago.
    But the rope would not.

69

She went a little farther and she calls to a rat,
Rat, rat, gnaw rope,
Rope won't hang butcher,
Butcher won't kill ox,
Ox won't drink water,
Water won't quench fire,
Fire won't burn stick,
Stick won't beat dog,
Dog won't bite pig,
Pig will not go,
And I should have been at home two hours ago.
    But the rat would not.

She went a little farther and she calls to a cat,
Cat, cat, kill rat,
Rat won't gnaw rope,
Rope won't hang butcher,
Butcher won't kill ox,
Ox won't drink water,
Water won't quench fire,
Fire won't burn stick,
Stick won't beat dog,
Dog won't bite pig,
Pig will not go,
And I should have been at home two hours ago.

Then the cat began to kill the rat,
The rat began to gnaw the rope,
The rope began to hang the butcher,
The butcher began to kill the ox,
The ox began to drink the water,
The water began to quench the fire,
The fire began to burn the stick,
The stick began to beat the dog,
The dog began to bite the pig,
The pig began to go;
    So it's all over, and the old woman's home again now.

THERE WAS AN OLD MAN

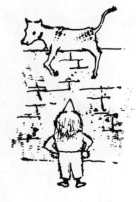

There was an old man,
And he had a calf,
  And that's half;
He took him out of the stall,
And put him on the wall,
And that's all.

TOMMY TUCKER

Little Tommy Tucker
  Sings for his supper:
What shall we give him?
  White bread and butter.
How shall he cut it
  Without e'er a knife?
How will he be married
  Without e'er a wife?

SULKY SUE

Here's Sulky Sue;
What shall we do?
Turn her face to the wall
Till she comes to.

THE MAN WITH NOUGHT

There was a man and he had nought,
　And robbers came to rob him;
He crept up to the chimney top,
　And then they thought they had
　　him.

But he got down on the other side,
　And then they could not find him;
He ran fourteen miles in fifteen days,
　And never looked behind him.

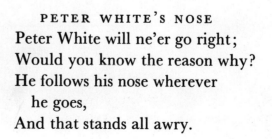

PETER WHITE'S NOSE

Peter White will ne'er go right;
Would you know the reason why?
He follows his nose wherever
　he goes,
And that stands all awry.

PEG

There was an old woman, her
    name was Peg;
Her head was of wood and she
    wore a cork leg.
The neighbours all pitched her
    into the water,
Her leg was drowned first, and
    her head followed after.

RAIN

Rain on the green grass,
    And rain on the tree,
Rain on the house-top,
    But not on me.

74

IT'S RAINING

It's raining, it's pouring,
The old man's snoring;
He got into bed
And bumped his head
And couldn't get up in the
    morning.

LITTLE BLUE BEN

Little Blue Ben, who lives in the glen,
Keeps a blue cat and one blue hen,
Which lays of blue eggs a score and ten;
Where shall I find the little Blue Ben?

THREE COOKS

There were three cooks of Colebrook,
And they fell out with our cook;
And all was for a pudding he took
From the three cooks of Colebrook.

75

CHARLIE WAG

Charlie Wag,
  Charlie Wag,
Ate the pudding
  And left the bag.

THE BIG BOY

When I was a little boy
  My mammy kept me in,
But now I am a big boy
  I'm fit to serve the king;
I can hand a musket,
  And I can smoke a pipe,
And I can kiss a bonny girl
  At twelve o'clock at night.

HANNAH BANTRY

Hannah Bantry,
  In the pantry,
Gnawing at a mutton bone;
  How she gnawed it,
  How she clawed it,
When she found herself alone.

HICKORY, DICKORY, DOCK

Hickory, dickory, dock,
The mouse ran up the clock.
  The clock struck one,
  The mouse ran down,
Hickory, dickory, dock.

GOOSE FEATHERS

Cackle, cackle, Mother Goose,
Have you any feathers loose?
Truly have I, pretty fellow,
Half enough to fill a pillow.
Here are quills, take one or two,
And down to make a bed for you.

COCK AND HEN

Cock: Lock the dairy door,
Lock the dairy door!
Hen: Chickle, chackle, chee,
I haven't got a key!

GOLDEN FISHES

When I was a little boy
I washed my mammy's dishes;
I put my finger in my eye,
And pulled out golden fishes.

BABY AND I

Baby and I
Were baked in a pie,
The gravy was wonderful hot.
We had nothing to pay
To the baker that day
And so we crept out of the pot.

GEORGIE PORGIE

Georgie Porgie, pudding and pie,
Kissed the girls and made them cry;
When the boys came out to play,
Georgie Porgie ran away.

THERE WAS A MONKEY

There was a monkey climbed a tree,
When he fell down, then down fell he.

There was a crow sat on a stone,
When he was gone, then there was none.

There was an old wife did eat an apple,
When she ate two, she ate a couple.

There was a horse going to the mill,
When he went on, he stood not still.

There was a butcher cut his thumb,
When it did bleed, then blood did come.

There was a lackey ran a race,
When he ran fast, he ran apace.

There was a cobbler clouting shoon,
When they were mended, they were done.

There was a navy went to Spain,
When it returned it came again.

THE LITTLE BLACK DOG

The little black dog ran round the
        house,
And set the bull a-roaring,
And drove the monkey in the boat,
Who set the oars a-rowing,
And scared the cock upon the rock,
Who cracked his throat with crowing.

THE CAT AND THE FIDDLE

Hey diddle, diddle,
The cat and the fiddle,
The cow jumped over the moon;
The little dog laughed
To see such sport,
And the dish ran away with
the spoon.

JEMMY DAWSON

Brave news is come to town,
　　Brave news is carried;
Brave news is come to town,
　　Jemmy Dawson's married.

First he got a porridge-pot,
　　Then he bought a ladle;
Then he got a wife and child,
　　And then he bought a cradle.

LITTLE HUSBAND

I had a little husband,
　　No bigger than my thumb;
I put him in a pint pot
　　And there I bade him drum.
I gave him some garters
　　To garter up his hose,
And a little silk handkerchief
　　To wipe his pretty nose.

TO THE BAT

Bat, bat, come under my hat,
And I'll give you a slice of bacon;
And when I bake, I'll give you a cake,
If I am not mistaken.

CHURNING

Come, butter, come,
Come, butter, come;
Peter stands at the gate
Waiting for a butter cake.
Come, butter, come.

TWO BIRDS

There were two birds sat on a stone,
Fa, la, la, la, lal, de;
One flew away, and then there was one,
Fa, la, la, la, lal, de;
The other flew after, and then there was none.
Fa, la, la, la, lal, de;
And so the poor stone was left all alone,
Fa, la, la, la, lal, de.

POLLY

Polly put the kettle on,
Polly put the kettle on,
Polly put the kettle on,
  We'll all have tea.

Sukey take it off again,
Sukey take it off again,
Sukey take it off again,
  They've all gone away.
      Or
Polly put the kettle on,
Sally blow the bellows strong,
Molly call the muffin man,
  We'll all have tea.

THE SMOKING STICK

Mother and Father and Uncle Dick
Went to London on a stick;
The stick broke and made a smoke,
And stifled all the London folk.

POLLY FLINDERS

Little Polly Flinders
Sat among the cinders,
Warming her pretty little toes;
Her mother came and caught her,
And whipped her little daughter
For spoiling her nice new clothes.

GINGER
Ginger, Ginger, broke the winder,
Hit the winder—Crack!
The baker came out to give 'im a clout
And landed on 'is back.

BLOW, WIND, BLOW
Blow, wind, blow!
And go, mill, go!
That the miller may grind his corn;
That the baker may take it,
And into bread make it,
And bring us a loaf in the morn.

A MAN IN THE WILDERNESS
A man in the wilderness asked me,
How many strawberries grow in the
    sea.
I answered him, as I thought good,
As many red herrings as swim in the wood.

THE MOCKING BIRD

Hush, little baby, don't say a word,
Papa's going to buy you a mocking bird.

If the mocking bird won't sing,
Papa's going to buy you a diamond ring.

If the diamond ring turns to brass,
Papa's going to buy you a looking-glass.

If the looking glass gets broke,
Papa's going to buy you a billy-goat.

If that billy goat runs away,
Papa's going to buy you another today.

SIX LITTLE MICE

Six little mice sat down to spin;
Pussy passed by and she peeped in.
What are you doing, my little men?
Weaving coats for gentlemen.
Shall I come in and cut off your threads?
No, no, Mistress Pussy, you'd bite off
    our heads.
Oh, no, I'll not; I'll help you to spin.
That may be so, but you don't come in.

DAVY DUMPLING

Davy Davy Dumpling,
    Boil him in the pot;
Sugar him and butter him,
    And eat him while he's hot.

90

THE APPLE TREE

As I went up the apple tree
All the apples fell on me;
Bake a pudding, bake a pie,
Send it up to John MacKay;
John MacKay is not in,
Send it up to the man in the moon.

MISSING COMMAS

I saw a fishpond all on fire
I saw a house bow to a squire
I saw a parson twelve feet high
I saw a cottage near the sky
I saw a balloon made of lead
I saw a coffin drop down dead
I saw two sparrows run a race
I saw two horses making lace
I saw a girl just like a cat
I saw a kitten wear a hat
I saw a man who saw these too
And said though strange
      they all were true.

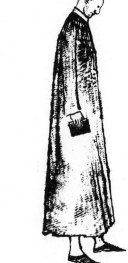

A SAD STORY

When I was a little boy
   I lived by myself,
And all the bread and cheese I got
   I laid upon a shelf.

The rats and the mice
   They made such a strife,
I had to go to London town
   And get me a wife.

The streets were so broad
   And the lanes were so narrow,
I was forced to bring my wife home
   In a wheelbarrow.

The wheelbarrow broke
   And my wife had a fall,
Farewell wheelbarrow,
   Little wife and all.

ROBIN-A-BOBBIN

Robin-A-Bobbin
He bent his bow,
Shot at a pigeon
And killed a crow;
Shot at another
And killed his own brother,
Did Robin-A-Bobbin
Who bent his bow.

ANNA MARIA

Anna Maria she sat on the fire;
The fire was too hot, she sat on the pot;
The pot was too round, she sat on the ground;
The ground was too flat, she sat on the cat;
The cat ran away with Maria on her back.

94

THREE BLIND MICE

Three blind mice, see how they run!
They all ran after the farmer's wife,
Who cut off their tails with a carving knife,
Did you ever see such a thing in your life,
  As three blind mice?

JOHNNIE NORRIE

Johnnie Norrie
Gaed up three paper stairies
And in at a paper doorie.

95

TOMMY O'LINN

Tommy O'Linn was a Scotsman born,
His head was bald and his beard was shorn:
He had a cap made of a hare's skin,
An alderman was Tommy O'Linn.

Tommy O'Linn had no boots to put on,
But two calves' skins with the hair all gone:
They were split at the side, and the water went in,
It's damp to the feet, said Tommy O'Linn.

Tommy O'Linn had no coat to put on,
He borrowed a goatskin to make himself one:
He planted the horns right under his chin,
They'll answer for pistols, said Tommy O'Linn.

Tommy O'Linn had no breeches to wear,
So he got him a sheepskin to make him a pair,
With the skinny side out and the woolly side in,
Aha! this is warm, said Tommy O'Linn.

Tommy O'Linn had no watch to put on,
So he scooped out a turnip to make himself one:
He caught a cricket, and put it within,
It is my own ticker, said Tommy O'Linn.

Tommy O'Linn went to bring his wife home,
He had but one horse that was all skin and bone:
I'll put her behind me as neat as a pin,
And her mother before me, said Tommy O'Linn.

Tommy O'Linn, his wife and wife's mother,
They all went over the bridge together:
The bridge broke down and they all tumbled in,
We'll find ground at the bottom, said Tommy O'Linn.

THE SQUIRREL

The winds they did blow,
   The leaves they did wag;
Along came a beggar boy,
   And put me in his bag.

He took me up to London,
   A lady did me buy,
Put me in a silver cage,
   And hung me up on high.

With apples by the fire,
   And nuts for to crack,
Besides a little feather bed
   To rest my little back.

CURLY LOCKS

Curly locks, Curly locks,
   Wilt thou be mine?
Thou shalt not wash dishes
   Nor yet feed the swine;
But sit on a cushion
   And sew a fine seam,
And feed upon strawberries,
   Sugar and cream.

IF WISHES WERE HORSES

If wishes were horses, beggars would
   ride.
If turnips were watches, I would
   wear one by my side.
   And if "ifs" and "ands"
   Were pots and pans,
There'd be no work for tinkers!

THE MAD MAN

There was a man, he went mad,
He jumped into a paper bag;
The paper bag was too narrow,
He jumped into a wheelbarrow;
The wheelbarrow took on fire,
He jumped into a cow byre;
The cow byre was too nasty,
He jumped into an apple pasty;
The apple pasty was too sweet,
He jumped into Chester-le-Street;
Chester-le-Street was full of stones,
He fell down and broke his bones.

IF ALL THE WORLD

If all the world was paper,
   And all the sea was ink,
If all the trees were bread and cheese,
   What should we have to drink?

99

THE EAGLE

Licenced to sell Beer, Ale, Wine, Spirits, Tobbacco

RICE 2ᴰ

BEST TREACLE

½ lb net

½

POP GOES THE WEASEL

Up and down the City Road,
　In and out the Eagle,
That's the way the money goes,
　Pop goes the weasel!

Half a pound of tuppenny rice,
　Half a pound of treacle,
Mix it up and make it nice,
　Pop goes the weasel!

Every night when I go out
　The monkey's on the table;
Take a stick and knock it off,
　Pop goes the weasel!

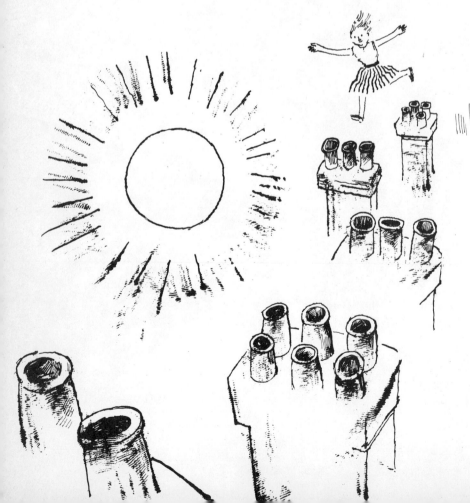

SALLY

Sally go round the sun,
Sally go round the moon,
Sally go round the chimney-pots
On a Saturday afternoon.

ROBIN THE BOBBIN

Robin the Bobbin,
 the big-bellied Ben,
He ate more meat
 than fourscore men;
He ate a cow,
 he ate a calf,
He ate a butcher
 and a half,
He ate a church,
 he ate a steeple,
He ate a priest
 and all the people!
A cow and a calf,
An ox and a half,
A church and a steeple,
And all the good people,
And yet he complained
 that his stomach wasn't full.

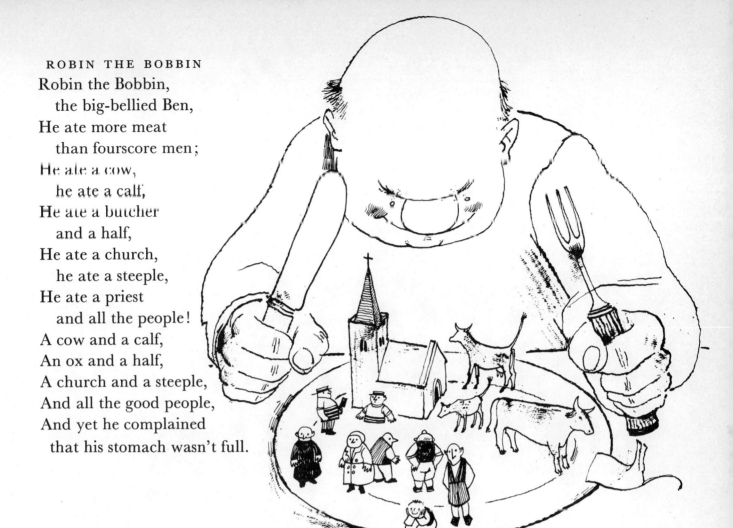

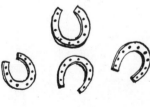

FOOT PATTING

Shoe a little horse,
Shoe a little mare,
But let the little colt
Go bare, bare, bare.

101

WHAT'S THE NEWS?
What's the news of the day,
Good neighbour, I pray?
They say the balloon
Is gone up to the moon.

THE SKY

Red sky at night,
Shepherd's delight;
Red sky in the morning,
Shepherd's warning.

TWO ROBINS

A robin and a robin's son
Once went to town to buy a bun.
They couldn't decide on plum or plain,
And so they went back home again.

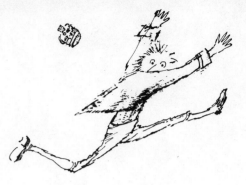

FOUR CHILDREN

William and Mary,
  George and Anne,
Four such children
  Had never a man:
They put their father
  To flight and shame,
And called their brother
  A shocking bad name.

THE SIMPLETON

When I was a little boy
   I had but little wit;
'Tis a long time ago,
   And I have no more yet;
Nor ever, ever shall,
   Until that I die,
For the longer I live
   The more fool am I.

TOMMY TITTLEMOUSE

Little Tommy Tittlemouse
Lived in a little house;
He caught fishes
In other men's ditches.

PETER

Peter, Peter, pumpkin eater,
Had a wife and couldn't keep her;
He put her in a pumpkin shell
And there he kept her very well.

CHARLEY BARLEY

Charley Barley, butter and eggs,
Sold his wife for three duck eggs.
When the ducks began to lay
Charley Barley flew away.

CAKES AND CUSTARD

When Jacky's a good boy,
   He shall have cakes and custard;
But when he does nothing but cry,
   He shall have nothing but mustard.

BABYLON

How many miles to Babylon?
Three-score and ten.
Can I get there by candle-light?
Yes, and back again.
If your heels are nimble and light,
You may get there by candle-light.

DADDY

Bring Daddy home
   With a fiddle and a drum,
A pocket full of spices,
   An apple and a plum.

THE COACHMAN

Up at Piccadilly oh!
   The coachman takes his stand,
And when he meets a pretty girl,
   He takes her by the hand;
   Whip away for ever oh!
   Drive away so clever oh!
   All the way to Bristol oh!
He drives her four-in-hand.

BARBER, BARBER

Barber, barber, shave a pig,
How many hairs will make a wig?
Four and twenty, that's enough.
Give the barber a pinch of snuff.

GOOD FRIDAY

Hot cross buns, hot cross buns;
One a penny poker,
Two a penny tongs,
Three a penny fire shovel,
Hot cross buns.

CHRISTMAS

Christmas comes but once a year,
And when it comes it brings good
   cheer,
A pocket full of money, and a cellar
   full of beer.

CHRISTMAS IS COMING

Christmas is coming,
   The geese are getting fat,
Please to put a penny
   In the old man's hat.
If you haven't got a penny,
   A ha'penny will do;
If you haven't got a ha'penny,
   Then God bless you!

HUMPTY DUMPTY

Humpty Dumpty sat on a wall,
Humpty Dumpty had a great fall;
All the King's horses and all the King's men
Couldn't put Humpty together again.

JEREMIAH

Jeremiah, blow the fire,
    Puff, puff, puff!
First you blow it gently,
    Then you blow it rough.

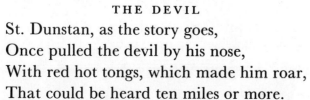

THE DEVIL

St. Dunstan, as the story goes,
Once pulled the devil by his nose,
With red hot tongs, which made him roar,
That could be heard ten miles or more.

THE LOVE-SICK FROG

A frog he would a-wooing go,
   Heigh ho! says Rowley,
Whether his mother would let him or no.

  With a rowley, powley, gammon and spinach,
   Heigh ho! says Anthony Rowley.

So off he set with his opera hat,
   Heigh ho! says Rowley,
And on the road he met with a rat.
With a rowley, powley, gammon and spinach,
   Heigh ho! says Anthony Rowley.

Pray, Mister Rat, will you go with me?
   Heigh ho! says Rowley,
Kind Mistress Mousey for to see?
  With a rowley, powley, gammon and spinach,
   Heigh ho! says Anthony Rowley.

They came to the door of Mousey's hall,
   Heigh ho! says Rowley,
They gave a loud knock, and they gave a loud call.
  With a rowley, powley, gammon and spinach,
   Heigh ho! says Anthony Rowley.

Pray, Mistress Mouse, are you within?
   Heigh ho! says Rowley,
Oh yes, kind sirs, I'm sitting to spin.
  With a rowley, powley, gammon and spinach,
   Heigh ho! says Anthony Rowley.

Pray, Mistress Mouse, will you give us some beer?
   Heigh ho! says Rowley,
For Froggy and I are fond of good cheer.
  With a rowley, powley, gammon and spinach,
   Heigh ho! says Anthony Rowley.

Pray, Master Frog, will you give us a song?
    Heigh ho! says Rowley,
Let it be something that's not very long.
    With a rowley, powley, gammon and spinach,
    Heigh ho! says Anthony Rowley.

Indeed, Mistress Mouse, replied Mister Frog,
    Heigh ho! says Rowley,
A cold has made me as hoarse as a dog.
    With a rowley, powley, gammon and spinach,
    Heigh ho! says Anthony Rowley.

Since you have a cold, Mister Frog, Mousey said,
    Heigh ho! says Rowley,
I'll sing you a song that I have just made.
    With a rowley, powley, gammon and spinach,
    Heigh ho! says Anthony Rowley.

But while they were all a-merry-making,
    Heigh ho! says Rowley,
A cat and her kittens came tumbling in.
    With a rowley, powley, gammon and spinach,
    Heigh ho! says Anthony Rowley.

The cat she seized the rat by the crown,
    Heigh ho! says Rowley,
The kittens they pulled the little mouse down.
With a rowley, powley, gammon and spinach,
    Heigh ho! says Anthony Rowley.

This put Mister Frog in a terrible fright,
    Heigh ho! says Anthony Rowley,
He took up his hat and he wished them good-night.
    With a rowley, powley, gammon and spinach,
    Heigh-ho! says Anthony Rowley.

But as Froggy was crossing over a brook,
    Heigh ho! says Rowley,
A lily-white duck came and gobbled him up.
    With a rowley, powley, gammon and spinach,
    Heigh ho! says Anthony Rowley.

THE RABBIT MAN

Here I am with my rabbits
Hanging on my pole,
The finest Hampshire rabbits
That e'er crept from a hole.

THE WISE MEN OF GOTHAM

Three wise men of Gotham
Went to sea in a bowl
If the bowl had been stronger,
My story would have been longer.

TO THE LADYBIRD

Ladybird, ladybird,
  Fly away home,
Your house is on fire
  And your children all gone;
All except one
  And that's little Ann
And she has crept under
  The warming pan.

HAY MAKING

Willy boy, Willy boy, where are you going?
I will go with you if that I may.
I'm going to the meadow to see them a-mowing,
I am going to help them to make the new hay.

LITTLE GIRL

Little girl, little girl,
  Where have you been?
I've been to see grandmother
  Over the green.
What did she give you?
  Milk in a can.
What did you say for it?
  Thank you, Grandam.

BOW-WOW

Bow-wow, says the dog,
Mew, mew, says the cat,
Grunt, grunt, goes the hog,
And squeak goes the rat.
Tu-whu, says the owl,
Caw, caw, says the crow,
Quack, quack, says the duck,
And what cuckoos say you know.

SNAIL HUNTERS

Four and twenty tailors
    Went to kill a snail,
The best man amongst them
    Durst not touch her tail;
She put out her horns
    Like a little Kyloe cow,
Run, tailors, run,
    Or she'll kill you all e'en now.

THE OWL

A wise old owl sat in an oak,
The more he heard the less he spoke;
The less he spoke the more he heard.
Why aren't we all like that wise old
      bird?

PEASE PORRIDGE

Pease porridge hot,
Pease porridge cold,
Pease porridge in the pot
Nine days old.
Some like it hot,
Some like it cold,
Some like it in the pot
Nine days old.

DING, DONG, BELL

Ding, dong, bell,
Pussy's in the well.
Who put her in?
Little Johnny Green.
Who pulled her out?
Little Tommy Stout.
What a naughty boy was that
To try to drown poor pussy cat,
Who never did him any harm,
And killed the mice in his father's
    barn.

PUTTING ON A NIGHTGOWN
Little man in coal pit
  Goes knock, knock, knock;
Up he comes, up he comes,
  Out at the top.

MARY'S LAMB
Mary had a little lamb,
  Its fleece was white as snow;
And everywhere that Mary went
  The lamb was sure to go.
It followed her to school one day,
  That was against the rule;
It made the children laugh and play
  To see a lamb at school.
And so the teacher turned it out,
  But still it lingered near,
And waited patiently about
  Till Mary did appear.
Why does the lamb love Mary so?
  The eager children cry;
Why, Mary loves the lamb, you know,
  The teacher did reply.

MY BLACK HEN
Hickety, pickety, my black hen,
She lays eggs for gentlemen;
Gentlemen come every day
To see what my black hen doth lay.

120

TO THE MAGPIE

Magpie, magpie, flutter and flee,
Turn up your tail and good luck
   come to me.

One for sorrow, two for joy,
Three for a girl, four for a boy,
Five for silver, six for gold,
Seven for a secret ne'er to be told.

THE FIRST OF MAY

The fair maid who, the First of May,
Goes to the fields at break of day,
And washes in dew from the hawthorn tree,
Will ever after handsome be.

TOMMY TROT

Tommy Trot, a man of law,
Sold his bed and lay upon straw;
Sold the straw and slept on grass,
To buy his wife a looking-glass.

THE QUEEN OF HEARTS

The Queen of Hearts
  She made some tarts,
All on a summer's day;
  The Knave of Hearts
  He stole those tarts,
And took them clean away.

The King of Hearts
  Called for the tarts,
And beat the knave full sore;
  The Knave of Hearts
  Brought back the tarts,
And vowed he'd steal no more.

MISSING COMMAS

I saw a pack of cards gnawing a bone
I saw a dog seated on Britain's throne
I saw a Queen shut up within a box
I saw a shilling driving a fat ox
I saw a man lying in a muff all night
I saw a glove reading news by candle-light
I saw a woman not a twelvemonth old
I saw a greatcoat all of solid gold
I saw two buttons telling of their dreams
I heard my friends, who wish'd I'd quit these themes.

TICKLY, TICKLY

Tickly, tickly, on your knee,
If you laugh you don't love me.

OLD CHAIRS

If I'd as much money as I could spend,
I never would cry, Old chairs to mend.
Old chairs to mend! Old chairs to mend!
I never would cry, Old chairs to mend.

JACKY JINGLE

Now what do you think
   Of little Jack Jingle?
Before he was married
   He used to live single.
But after he married,
   To alter his life,
He left off living single
   And lived with his wife.

SING, SING

Sing, sing,
   What shall I sing?
The cat's run away
   With the pudding string!

Do, do,
   What shall I do?
The cat's run away
   With the pudding too!

COCK A DOODLE DOO

Cock a doodle doo!
My dame has lost her shoe,
My master's lost his fiddling stick
And knows not what to do.

Cock a doodle doo!
What is my dame to do?
Till master finds his fiddling stick
She'll dance without her shoe.

Cock a doodle doo!
My dame has found her shoe,
And master's found his fiddling stick,
Sing doodle doodle doo.

Cock a doodle doo!
My dame will dance with you,
While master fiddles his fiddling stick
For dame and doodle doo.

JACK HORNER

Little Jack Horner
Sat in the corner,
Eating his Christmas pie;
He put in his thumb,
And pulled out a plum,
And said, What a good boy am I!

LONDON BRIDGE

London Bridge is broken down,
  Broken down, broken down,
London Bridge is broken down,
  My fair lady.

Build it up with wood and clay,
  Wood and clay, wood and clay,
Build it up with wood and clay,
  My fair lady.

Wood and clay will wash away,
  Wash away, wash away,
Wood and clay will wash away,
  My fair lady.

Build it up with bricks and mortar,
  Bricks and mortar, bricks and
    mortar,
Build it up with bricks and mortar,
  My fair lady.

Bricks and mortar will not stay,
  Will not stay, will not stay,
Bricks and mortar will not stay,
  My fair lady.

Build it up with iron and steel,
  Iron and steel, iron and steel,
Build it up with iron and steel,
  My fair lady.

Iron and steel will bend and bow,
  Bend and bow, bend and bow,
Iron and steel will bend and bow,
  My fair lady.

Build it up with silver and gold,
  Silver and gold, silver and gold,
Build it up with silver and gold,
  My fair lady.

Silver and gold will be stolen away,
  Stolen away, stolen away,
Silver and gold will be stolen away,
  My fair lady.

Set a man to watch all night,
  Watch all night, watch all night,
Set a man to watch all night,
  My fair lady.

Suppose the man should fall asleep,
  Fall asleep, fall asleep,
Suppose the man should fall asleep,
  My fair lady.

Give him a pipe to smoke all night,
  Smoke all night, smoke all night,
Give him a pipe to smoke all night,
  My fair lady.

PUSSY CAT

Pussy cat ate the dumplings,
Pussy cat ate the dumplings,
   Mamma stood by,
   And cried, Oh, fie!
Why did you eat the dumplings?

RUN, BOYS, RUN

Rats in the garden, catch 'em Towser,
Cows in the cornfield, run, boys, run;
Cat's in the cream pot, stop her, now sir,
Fire on the mountain, run, boys, run.

THE MISCHIEVOUS RAVEN

A farmer went trotting upon his grey mare,
    Bumpety, bumpety, bump!
With his daughter behind him so rosy and fair,
    Lumpety, lumpety, lump!

A raven cried, Croak! and they all tumbled down,
    Bumpety, bumpety, bump!
The mare broke her knees and the farmer his crown,
    Lumpety, lumpety, lump!

The mischievous raven flew laughing away,
    Bumpety, bumpety, bump!
And vowed he would serve them the same the next day,
    Lumpety, lumpety, lump!

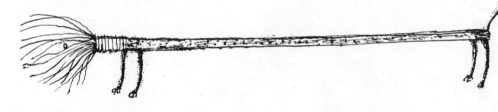

HIGGLETY, PIGGLETY

Higglety, pigglety, pop!
The dog has eaten the mop;
    The pig's in a hurry,
    The cat's in a flurry,
Higglety, pigglety, pop!

ROBIN AND RICHARD

Robin and Richard
  Were two pretty men,
They lay in bed
  Till the clock struck ten;
Then up starts Robin
  And looks at the sky,
Oh, brother Richard,
  The sun's very high.
You go before
  With the bottle and bag,
And I will come after
  On little Jack Nag.

ADVICE

He that would thrive
Must rise at five;
He that hath thriven
May lie till seven;
He that will never thrive
May lie till eleven.

131

A NAIL

For want of a nail
  The shoe was lost,
For want of a shoe
  The horse was lost,
For want of a horse
  The rider was lost,
For want of a rider
  The battle was lost,
For want of a battle
  The kingdom was lost,
And all for the want
  Of a horse shoe nail.

LUCY AND KITTY

Lucy Locket lost her pocket,
  Kitty Fisher found it;
Not a penny was there in it,
  Only ribbon round it.

THE KEY OF THE KINGDOM

This is the key of the kingdom:
In that kingdom is a city,
In that city is a town,
In that town there is a street,
In that street there winds a lane,
In that lane there is a yard,
In that yard there is a house,
In that house there waits a room,
In that room there is a bed,
On that bed there is a basket,
   A basket of flowers.

Flowers in the basket,
Basket on the bed,
Bed in the chamber,
Chamber in the house,
House in the weedy yard,
Yard in the winding lane,
Lane in the broad street,
Street in the high town,
Town in the city,
City in the kingdom:
   This is the key of the kingdom.

DAME TROT

Dame Trot and her cat
   Sat down for a chat;
The Dame sat on this side
   And puss sat on that.

Puss, says the Dame,
   Can you catch a rat,
Or a mouse in the dark?
   Purr, says the cat.

PUNCTUALITY

First in a carriage,
   Second in a gig,
Third on a donkey,
   And fourth on a pig.

OLD BONIFACE

Old Boniface he loved good cheer,
  And took his glass of Burton,
And when the nights grew sultry hot
  He slept without a shirt on.

RABBIT SKIN

Bye, baby bunting,
Daddy's gone a-hunting,
Gone to get a rabbit skin
To wrap the baby bunting in.

JACK-A-DANDY

Nauty Pauty Jack-a-Dandy
Stole a piece of sugar candy
From the grocer's shoppy-shop,
And away did hoppy-hop.

FIVE HENS

There was an old man who lived in Middle Row,
He had five hens and a name for them, oh!
Bill and Ned and Battock,
Cut-her-foot and Pattock,
Chuck, my lady Pattock,
Go to thy nest and lay.

BANDY LEGS
As I was going to sell my eggs
I met a man with bandy legs,
Bandy legs and crooked toes;
I tripped up his heels, and he
    fell on his nose.

TO MARKET
To market, to market,
    To buy a plum bun;
Home again, home again,
    Market is done.

GOODNIGHT
Good night, sweet repose,
Half the bed and all the clothes.

OH DEAR!
Dear, dear! what can the matter be?
Two old women got up in an apple-
    tree;
One came down, and the other
    stayed till Saturday.

A was an
Apple pie

B
Bit it

C
Cut it

D
Dealt it

E
Eat it

F
Fought for it

G
Got it

H
Had it

I
Inspected it

J
Joined for it

K
Kept it

L
Longed for it

M
Mourned for it

N
Nodded at it

O
Opened it

P
Peeped in it

Q
Quartered it

R
Ran for it

S
Stole it

T
Took it

U
Upset it

V
Viewed it

W
Wanted it

XYZ and &
All wished for
a piece in hand

137

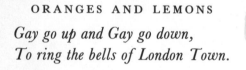

ORANGES AND LEMONS

Gay go up and Gay go down,
To ring the bells of London Town.

Bull's eyes and targets,
Say the bells of St. Marg'ret's.

Brickbats and tiles,
Say the bells of St. Giles'.

Oranges and lemons,
Say the bells of St. Clement's.

Pancakes and fritters,
Say the bells of St. Peter's.

Two sticks and an apple,
Say the bells at Whitechapel.

Old Father Baldpate,
Say the slow bells at Aldgate.

Maids in white aprons,
Say the bells at St. Catherine's.

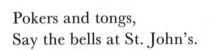

Pokers and tongs,
Say the bells at St. John's.

Kettles and pans,
Say the bells at St. Anne's.

You owe me five farthings,
Say the bells of St. Martin's.

When will you pay me?
Say the bells at Old Bailey.

When I grow rich,
Say the bells at Shoreditch.

Pray, when will that be?
Say the bells at Stepney.

I'm sure I don't know,
Says the great bell at Bow.

Here comes a candle to light you to bed,
Here comes a chopper to chop off your head.

SOLOMON GRUNDY

Solomon Grundy,
Born on a Monday,
Christened on Tuesday,
Married on Wednesday,
Took ill on Thursday,
Worse on Friday,
Died on Saturday,
Buried on Sunday.
This is the end
Of Solomon Grundy.

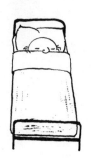

THE FINGERS

Tom Thumbkin,
Willie Wilkin,
Long Daniel,
Betty Bodkin,
And Little Dick.

MRS MASON'S BASIN

Mrs Mason bought a basin,
Mrs Tyson said, What a nice 'un,
What did it cost? said Mrs Frost,
Half a crown, said Mrs Brown,
Did it indeed, said Mrs Reed,
It did for certain, said Mrs Burton.
Then Mrs Nix up to her tricks
Threw the basin on the bricks.

PIPPEN HILL

As I was going up Pippen Hill,
  Pippen Hill was dirty.
There I met a pretty miss
  And she dropt me a curtsey.

Little miss, pretty miss,
  Blessings light upon you!
If I had half a crown a day,
  I'd spend it all upon you.

THE LADY AND THE SWINE

There was a lady loved a swine,
  Honey, quoth she,
Pig-hog wilt thou be mine?
  Hoogh, quoth he.

I'll build thee a silver sty,
    Honey, quoth she,
And in it thou shalt lie.
    Hoogh, quoth he.

Pinned with a silver pin,
    Honey, quoth she,
That thou may go out and in.
    Hoogh, quoth he.

Wilt thou have me now,
    Honey? quoth she.
Speak or my heart will break.
    Hoogh, quoth he.

ROCK-A-BYE

Rock-a-bye, baby,
  Thy cradle is green,
Father's a nobleman,
  Mother's a queen;
And Betty's a lady,
  And wears a gold ring;
And Johnny's a drummer,
  And drums for the king.

THE RECRUITING SERGEANT

Come here to me, my merry, merry men,
  Said a sergeant at the fair;
And the bumpkins all were very merry men,
  And they all came running there.
Fat and spare, round and square,
  See them stare with noddles bare,
And the piper piped an air,
  And the drummer drummed his share,
With a rub-a-dub, rub-a-dub, row dow dow,
And the little dogs answered bow, wow, wow,
  And the boys cried out Hurrah!
Hurrah! Hurrah! Hurrah!

OLD ROGER

Old Roger is dead and laid in his grave,
  Laid in his grave, laid in his grave;
Old Roger is dead and laid in his grave,
  H'm ha! laid in his grave.

They planted an apple tree over his head,
  Over his head, over his head,
They planted an apple tree over his head,
  H'm ha! over his head.

The apples grew ripe and ready to fall,
  Ready to fall, ready to fall;
The apples grew ripe and ready to fall,
  H'm ha! ready to fall.

There came an old woman a-picking them all,
  A-picking them all, a-picking them all;
There came an old woman a-picking them all,
  H'm ha! picking them all.

Old Roger jumps up and gives her a knock,
  Gives her a knock, gives her a knock;
Which makes the old woman go hipperty-hop,
  H'm ha! hipperty-hop.

THE DERBY RAM

As I was going to Derby
    Upon a market day,
I met the finest ram, sir,
    That ever was fed on hay.

This ram was fat behind, sir,
    This ram was fat before,
This ram was three yards high, sir,
    Indeed he was no more.

The wool upon his back, sir,
    Reached up unto the sky,
The eagles built their nests there,
    For I heard the young ones cry.

The wool upon his tail, sir,
    Was three yards and an ell,
Of it they made a rope, sir,
    To pull the parish bell.

The space between the horns, sir,
    Was as far as man could reach,
And there they built a pulpit,
    But no one in it preached.

This ram had four legs to walk upon,
    This ram had four legs to stand,
And every leg he had, sir,
    Stood on an acre of land.

Now the man that fed the ram, sir,
    He fed him twice a day,
And each time that he fed him, sir,
    He ate a rick of hay.

The man that killed the ram, sir,
    Was up to his knees in blood,
And the boy that held the pail, sir,
    Was carried away in the flood.

Indeed, sir, it's the truth, sir,
    For I never was taught to lie,
And if you go to Derby, sir,
    You may eat a bit of the pie.

AN OLD WOMAN

There was an old woman tossed up in a basket,
  Seventeen times as high as the moon;
Where she was going I couldn't but ask it,
  For in her hand she carried a broom.

Old woman, old woman, old woman, quoth I,
Where are you going to up so high?
To brush the cobwebs off the sky!
May I go with you? Aye, by-and-by.

HINX, MINX

Hinx, minx, the old witch winks,
The fat begins to fry,
Nobody at home but Jumping Joan,
Father, Mother, and I.
Stick, stock, stone dead,
Blind man can't see;
Every knave will have a slave,
You or I must be he.

TWO LITTLE BLACKBIRDS

As I went over the water,
  The water went over me.
I saw two little blackbirds
  Sitting on a tree;
One called me a rascal,
  And one called me a thief,
I took up my little black stick
  And knocked out all their
    teeth.

GREAT A

Great A, little a,
    Bouncing B,
The cat's in the cupboard
    And can't see me.

COBBLER, COBBLER

Cobbler, cobbler, mend my shoe,
Get it done by half past two;
Stitch it up, and stitch it down,
Then I'll give you half a crown.

OLD KING COLE

Old King Cole
Was a merry old soul,
And a merry old soul was he;
He called for his pipe,
And he called for his bowl,
And he called for his fiddlers three.

Every fiddler he had a fiddle,
And a very fine fiddle had he;
Oh, there's none so rare
As can compare
With King Cole and his fiddlers three.

147

CHERRY STONES

Tinker,   Tailor,   Soldier,   Sailor,   Rich man,   Poor man, Beggar man, Thief.

Lady,
Baby,
Gipsy,
Queen.

SPRING
March winds and April showers
Bring forth May flowers.

THE LITTLE NUT TREE
I had a little nut tree,
   Nothing would it bear
But a silver nutmeg
   And a golden pear;
The king of Spain's daughter
   Came to visit me,
And all for the sake
   Of my little nut tree.

ONE, TWO, THREE, FOUR, FIVE
One, two, three, four, five,
Once I caught a fish alive,
Six, seven, eight, nine, ten,
Then I let it go again.
Why did you let it go?
Because it bit my finger so.
Which finger did it bite?
The little finger on the right.

RIDE A COCK-HORSE
Ride a cock-horse to Banbury Cross,
To see a fine lady upon a white horse;
Rings on her fingers and bells on her toes,
And she shall have music wherever
    she goes.

MY MAID MARY
My maid Mary,
  She minds the dairy,
While I go a-hoeing and mowing each morn;
  Merrily run the reel,
    And the little spinning wheel,
Whilst I am singing and mowing my corn.

149

TERENCE MCDIDDLER

Terence McDiddler,
  The three-stringed fiddler,
Can charm, if you please,
  The fish from the seas.

TEE-WEE'S BOAT

Little Tee-wee,
He went to sea,
In an open boat;
And when it was afloat,
The little boat bended,
My story's ended.

BOBBY SHAFTOE

Bobby Shaftoe's gone to sea,
Silver buckles at his knee;
He'll come back and marry me,
   Bonny Bobby Shaftoe

Bobby Shaftoe's bright and fair,
Combing down his yellow hair,
He's my ain for evermair,
   Bonny Bobby Shaftoe.

Bobby Shaftoe's tall and slim,
He's always dressed so neat and trim,
The ladies they all keek at him,
   Bonny Bobby Shaftoe.

Bobby Shaftoe's getten a bairn
For to dandle in his arm;
In his arm and on his knee,
   Bobby Shaftoe loves me.

A PRETTY MAID

Ickle ockle, blue bockle,
  Fishes in the sea,
If you want a pretty maid,
  Please choose me.

THE WIND
When the wind is in the east,
'Tis neither good for man nor beast;
When the wind is in the north,
The skilful fisher goes not forth;
When the wind is in the south,
It blows the bait in the fishes' mouth;
When the wind is in the west,
Then 'tis at the very best.

TEN O'CLOCK SCHOLAR
A diller, a dollar,
A ten o'clock scholar,
What makes you come so soon?
You used to come at ten o'clock,
But now you come at noon.

THE BEGGARS

Hark, hark,
The dogs do bark,
The beggars are coming to town;
Some in rags,
And some in jags,
And one in a velvet gown.

CONTRARY MARY

Mary, Mary, quite contrary,
How does your garden grow?
With silver bells and cockle shells,
And pretty maids all in a row.

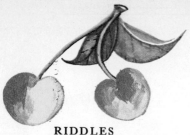

RIDDLES

Riddle me, riddle me ree,
A little man in a tree;
A stick in his hand,
A stone in his throat,
If you read me this riddle
I'll give you a groat.

Little Nancy Etticoat,
With a white petticoat,
And a red nose;
She has no feet or hands,
The longer she stands
The shorter she grows.

Black I am and much admired,
Men seek for me until they're tired;
When they find me, break my head,
And take me from my resting bed.

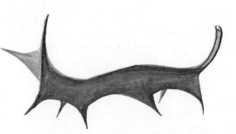

Highty tighty, paradighty,
Clothed all in green,
The king could not read it,
No more could the queen;
They sent for the wise men
From out of the East,
Who said it had horns,
But was not a beast.

A house full, a hole full,
And you cannot gather a bowl full.

Thirty white horses
Upon a red hill,
Now they stamp,
Now they champ,
Now they stand still.

I'm called by the name of a man,
Yet am as little as a mouse;
When winter comes I love to be
With my red target near the house.

In marble walls as white as milk,
Lined with a skin as soft as silk,
Within a fountain crystal-clear,
A golden apple doth appear.
No doors there are to this stronghold,
Yet thieves break in and steal the gold.

Clothed in yellow, red, and green,
I prate before the king and queen;
Of neither house nor land possessed,
By lords and knights I am caressed.

Flour of England, fruit of Spain,
Met together in a shower of rain;
Put in a bag, tied round with a string;
If you tell me this riddle,
I'll give you a ring.

Black within, and red without,
Four corners round about.

Around the rick, around the rick,
And there I found my Uncle Dick.
I screwed his neck,
I sucked his blood,
And left his body lying.

In Spring I look gay,
Decked in comely array,
In Summer more clothing I wear;
When colder it grows,
I fling off my clothes,
And in Winter quite naked appear.

Two brothers we are,
Great burdens we bear,
On which we are bitterly pressed;
The truth is to say,
We are full all the day,
And empty when we go to rest.

Purple, yellow, red, and green,
The king cannot reach it, nor yet the queen;
Nor can Old Noll, whose power's so great:
Tell me this riddle while I count eight.

As I was going o'er London Bridge,
I heard something crack;
Not a man in all England
Can mend that.

The land was white,
The seed was black;
It will take a good scholar
To riddle me that.

I have a little sister, they call her
Peep-Peep,
She wades the waters deep, deep, deep;
She climbs the mountains high, high,
high;
Poor little creature she has but one eye.

He went to the wood and caught it,
He sat him down and sought it;
Because he could not find it,
Home with him he brought it.

Two legs sat upon three legs
With one leg in his lap;
In comes four legs
And runs away with one leg;
Up jumps two legs,
Catches up three legs,
Throws it after four legs,
And makes him bring back one leg.

Little Billy Breek
Sits by the reek,
He has more horns
Than all the king's sheep.

Higher than a house,
Higher than a tree,
Oh, whatever can that be?

As round as an apple,
As deep as a cup,
And all the king's horses
Cannot pull it up.

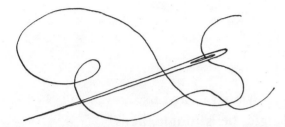

Old Mother Twitchett has but one eye,
And a long tail which she can let fly,
And every time she goes over a gap,
She leaves a bit of her tail in a trap.

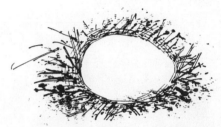

As I was walking in a field of wheat,
I picked up something good to eat;
Neither fish, flesh, fowl, nor bone,
I kept it till it ran alone.

Goes through the mud,
And through the mud,
And only leaves one track.

There was a thing a full month old
When Adam was no more;
Before the thing was five weeks old
Adam was years four score.

Four stiff-standers,
Four dilly-danders,
Two lookers,
Two crookers,
And a wig-wag.

JINGLE BELLS

Jingle, bells! jingle, bells!
　　Jingle all the way;
Oh, what fun it is to ride
　　In a one-horse open sleigh.

THE MILKMAN

Milkman, milkman, where have you been?
In Buttermilk Channel up to my chin;
I spilt my milk, and I spoilt my clothes,
And got a long icicle hung from my nose.

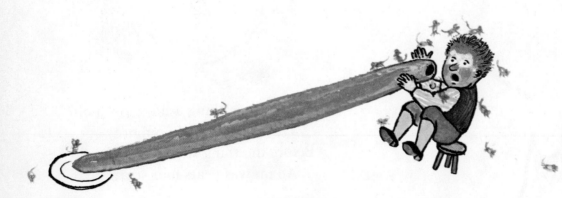

THE PASTY

Deedle deedle dumpling, my son John,
Ate a pasty five feet long;
He bit it once, he bit it twice,
Oh, my goodness, it was full of mice!

MY MOTHER SAID

My mother said, I never should
Play with the gypsies in the wood.
If I did, then she would say:
Naughty girl to disobey.
Your hair shan't curl and your shoes shan't shine,
You gypsy girl you shan't be mine.
And my father said that if I did,
He'd rap my head with the teapot lid.
My mother said that I never should
Play with the gypsies in the wood.
The wood was dark, the grass was green;
By came Sally with a tambourine.
I went to sea—no ship to get across;
I paid ten shillings for a blind white horse.
I upped on his back and was off in a crack,
Sally tell my mother I shall never come back.

JOHN BULL

John Bull, John Bull,
Your belly's so full,
You can't jump over
A three-legged stool.

LITTLE BO-PEEP

Little Bo-peep has lost her sheep,
    And doesn't know where to find them;
Leave them alone, and they'll come home,
    Bringing their tails behind them.

Little Bo-peep fell fast asleep,
    And dreamt she heard them bleating;
But when she awoke, she found it a joke,
    For they were still a-fleeting.

Then up she took her little crook,
    Determined for to find them;
She found them indeed, but it made her heart bleed,
    For they'd left their tails behind them.

It happened one day, as Bo-peep did stray
    Into a meadow hard by,
There she espied their tails side by side,
    All hung on a tree to dry.

She heaved a sigh, and wiped her eye,
    And over the hillocks went rambling,
And tried what she could, as a shepherdess should,
    To tack again each to its lambkin.

CUCKOO, CHERRY TREE

Cuckoo, cuckoo, cherry tree,
Catch a bird, and give it me;
Let the tree be high or low,
Let it hail or rain or snow.

WHITE CAP

See-saw, down in my lap,
    Up again onto her feet;
Little girl lost her white cap,
    Blown away in the street.

THE OLD WOMAN IN A SHOE

There was an old woman who lived in a shoe,
She had so many children she didn't know
   what to do;
She gave them some broth without any bread;
She whipped them all soundly and put them
   to bed.

CROSS-PATCH

Cross-patch,
Draw the latch,
Sit by the fire and spin;
Take a cup,
And drink it up,
Then call your neighbours in.

HODDLEY, PODDLEY

Hoddley, poddley, puddle and fogs,
Cats are to marry the poodle dogs;
Cats in blue jackets and dogs in red
    hats,
What will become of the mice and
    the rats?

YANKEE DOODLE

Yankee Doodle came to town,
    Riding on a pony;
He stuck a feather in his cap
And called it macaroni.

RED STOCKINGS

Red stockings, blue stockings,
Shoes tied up with silver;
A red rosette upon my breast
And a gold ring on my finger.

TUPPENCE HA'PENNY FARDEN

The rose is red, the rose is white,
    The rose is in my garden;
I would not part with my sweetheart
    For tuppence ha'penny farden.

PUSSY CAT

Pussy cat, pussy cat,
    Where have you been?
I've been to London
    To look at the Queen.
Pussy cat, pussy cat,
    What did you there?
I frightened a little mouse
    Under her chair.

163

THE CARRION CROW

A carrion crow sat on an oak,
Watching a tailor shape his cloak.
    Sing heigh ho, the carrion crow,
    Fol de riddle, lol de riddle, hi ding do.

The carrion crow began to rave,
And called the tailor a crooked knave.
    Sing heigh ho, the carrion crow,
    Fol de riddle, lol de riddle, hi ding do.

Wife, bring me my old bent bow,
That I may shoot yon carrion crow.
    Sing heigh ho, the carrion crow,
    Fol de riddle, lol de riddle, hi ding do.

The tailor he shot and missed his mark,
And shot his own sow through the heart.
    Sing heigh ho, the carrion crow,
    Fol de riddle, lol de riddle, hi ding do.

Wife, bring brandy in a spoon,
For our old sow is in a swoon.
    Sing heigh ho, the carrion crow,
    Fol de riddle, lol de riddle, hi ding do.

MY FIRST SUITOR

Little Jack Dandy-prat
 Was my first suitor;
He had a dish and spoon
 And a little pewter;
He'd linen and woollen,
 And woollen and linen,
A little pig on a string
 Cost him five shilling.

ELSIE MARLEY

Elsie Marley is grown so fine,
She won't get up to feed the swine,
But lies in bed till eight or nine.
 Lazy Elsie Marley.

A PROPOSAL

Sukey, you shall be my wife
 And I will tell you why:
I have got a little pig,
 And you have got a sty;
I have got a dun cow,
 And you can make good cheese;
Sukey, will you marry me?
 Say Yes, if you please.

GIANT BONAPARTE

Baby, baby, naughty baby,
Hush, you squalling thing, I say.
Peace this moment, peace, or maybe
Bonaparte will pass this way.

Baby, baby, he's a giant,
Tall and black as Rouen steeple,
And he breakfasts, dines, rely on't,
Every day on naughty people.

Baby, baby, if he hears you,
As he gallops past the house,
Limb from limb at once he'll tear you,
Just as pussy tears a mouse.

And he'll beat you, beat you, beat you,
And he'll beat you all to pap,
And he'll eat you, eat you, eat you,
Every morsel snap, snap, snap.

MOON

Moon, moon,
Mak' me a pair o'shoon,
And I'll dance till you be done.

SATURDAY NIGHT

On Saturday night I lost my wife,
And where do you think I found her?
Up in the moon, singing a tune,
And all the stars around her.

IN THE DUMPS

We are all in the dumps,
For diamonds are trumps,
The kittens are gone to St. Paul's.
The babies are bit,
The moon's in a fit,
And the houses are built without
walls.

167

THE RIOT

The sow came in with the saddle,
The little pig rocked the cradle,
The dish jumped up on the table
To see the pot swallow the ladle.
The spit that stood behind the door
Threw the pudding-stick on the floor
  Odd's-bobs! says the gridiron,
    Can't you agree?
I'm the head constable,
  Bring them to me.

KING ARTHUR

When good King Arthur ruled this land,
  He was a goodly King;
He stole three pecks of barley-meal
  To make a bag-pudding.

A bag-pudding the King did make,
  And stuffed it well with plums,
And in it put great lumps of fat,
  As big as my two thumbs.

The King and Queen did eat thereof,
  And noblemen beside;
And what they could not eat that night,
  The Queen next morning fried.

A MAN OF DOUBLE DEED

There was a man of double deed
Sowed his garden full of seed.
When the seed began to grow,
'Twas like a garden full of snow;
When the snow began to melt,
'Twas like a ship without a belt;
When the ship began to sail,
'Twas like a bird without a tail;
When the bird began to fly,
'Twas like an eagle in the sky;
When the sky began to roar,
'Twas like a lion at the door;
When the door began to crack,
'Twas like a stick across my back;
When my back began to smart,
'Twas like a penknife in my heart;
When my heart began to bleed,
'Twas death and death and death indeed.

WOODEN HILL

Up the wooden hill
 to Bedfordshire,
Down Sheet Lane
 to Blanket Fair.

AN UNKIND LASS

It's once I courted as pretty a lass,
 As ever your eyes did see;
But now she's come to such a pass,
 She never will do for me.
She invited me to her house,
 Where oft I'd been before,
And she tumbled me into the hog-tub,
 And I'll never go there any more.

169

DOWN BY THE RIVER

Down by the river
  Where the green grass grows
Pretty Polly Perkins
  Bleaches her clothes.
She laughs and she sings,
  And she sings so sweet.
She calls, Come over,
  Across the street.
He kissed her, he kissed her,
  He took her to the town;
He bought her a ring
  And a damascene gown.

A COTTAGE IN FIFE

In a cottage in Fife
  Lived a man and his wife,
Who, believe me, were comical folk:
  For, to people's surprise,
  They both saw with their eyes,
And their tongues moved whenever they spoke.
  When quite fast asleep,
  I've been told that to keep
Their eyes open they could not contrive;
  They walked on their feet,
  And 'twas thought what they eat
Helped, with drinking, to keep them alive.

JOLLY MILLER

There was a jolly miller once,
  Lived on the river Dee;
He worked and sang from morn till
    night,
  No lark more blithe than he.
And this the burden of his song
  Forever used to be,
I care for nobody, no! not I,
  If nobody cares for me.

GREEN GRASS

A dis, a dis, a green grass,
  A dis, a dis, a dis;
Come all you pretty fair maids
  And dance along with us.

For we are going a-roving,
  A-roving in this land;
We'll take this pretty fair maid,
  We'll take her by the hand.

You shall have a duck, my dear,
  And you shall have a drake;
And you shall have a young prince,
  A young prince for your sake.

And if this young prince chance to
    die,
  You shall have another;
The bells will ring, and the birds will
    sing,
  And we'll all clap hands together.

A LITTLE COCK SPARROW

A little cock sparrow sat on a green
  tree,
And he chirruped, he chirruped, so merry
  was he.
A naughty boy came with his wee bow
  and arrow,
Says he, I will shoot this little cock
  sparrow.
His body will make me a nice little stew,
And his giblets will make me a little pie
  too.
Oh, no, said the sparrow, I won't make
  a stew,
So he clapped his wings and away he flew.

TWO PIGEONS

I had two pigeons bright and gay,
They flew from me the other day;
What was the reason they did go?
I cannot tell for I do not know.

PINS

See a pin and pick it up,
All the day you'll have good luck.
See a pin and let it lay,
Bad luck you'll have all the day.

DAYS IN THE MONTH

Thirty days hath September,
April, June, and November;
All the rest have thirty-one,
Excepting February alone,
And that has twenty-eight days clear
And twenty-nine in each leap year.

STAR LIGHT

Star light, star bright,
First star I see tonight,
I wish I may, I wish I might,
Have the wish I wish tonight.

GOING TO ST IVES

As I was going to St Ives,
I met a man with seven wives;
Each wife had seven sacks,
Each sack had seven cats,
Each cat had seven kits:
Kits, cats, sacks, and wives,
How many were there going to St Ives?

(One or None)

RING-A-RING O' ROSES

Ring-a-ring o' roses,
A pocket full of posies,
   A-tishoo! A-tishoo!
We all fall down.

The cows are in the meadow
Lying fast asleep,
   A-tishoo! A-tishoo!
We all get up again.

Or this way

A ring, a ring o' roses,
A pocket full of posies,
   Ash-a! Ash-a!
All stand still.

The king has sent his daughter
To fetch a pail of water,
   Ash-a! Ash-a!
All bow down.

The bird upon the steeple
Sits high above the people,
   Ash-a! Ash-a!
All kneel down.

The wedding bells are ringing,
The boys and girls are singing,
   Ash-a! Ash-a!
All fall down.

RACE STARTING

Bell horses, bell horses,
   What time of day?
One o'clock, two o'clock,
   Three and away.

One to make ready,
   And two to prepare;
Good luck to the rider,
   And away goes the mare.

One for money,
   Two for show,
Three to make ready,
   And four to go.

A PRAYER

Now I lay me down to sleep,
I pray the Lord my soul to keep;
And if I die before I wake,
I pray the Lord my soul to take.

A SHIP A-SAILING

I saw a ship a-sailing,
  A-sailing on the sea,
And oh, but it was laden
  With pretty things for thee!

There were comfits in the cabin,
  And apples in the hold;
The sails were made of silk,
  And the masts were all of gold.

The four-and-twenty sailors,
  That stood between the decks,
Were four-and-twenty white mice
  With chains about their necks.

The captain was a duck
  With a packet on his back,
And when the ship began to move
  The captain said, Quack! Quack!

IF

If all the seas were one sea,
What a *great* sea that would be!
If all the trees were one tree,
What a *great* tree that would be!
And if all the axes were one axe,
What a *great* axe that would be!
And if all the men were one man,
What a *great* man that would be!
And if the *great* man took the *great* axe,
And cut down the *great* tree,
And let it fall into the *great* sea,
What a splish-splash that would be!

KINDNESS

I love little pussy,
 Her coat is so warm,
And if I don't hurt her
 She'll do me no harm.
So I'll not pull her tail,
 Nor drive her away,
But pussy and I
 Very gently will play.
She shall sit by my side,
 And I'll give her some food;
And pussy will love me
 Because I am good.

WHAT'S IN THERE?

What's in there?
Gold and money.
Where's my share?
The mousie's run away
 with it.
Where's the mousie?
In her housie.
Where's her housie?
In the wood.
Where's the wood?
The fire burnt it.
Where's the fire?
The water quenched it.
Where's the water?
The brown bull drank it.
Where's the brown bull?
Behind Burnie's hill.
Where's Burnie's hill?
All dressed in snow.
Where's the snow?
The sun melted it.
Where's the sun?
High, high up in the air.

JACK A NORY

I'll tell you a story
About Jack a Nory,
And now my story's begun;
I'll tell you another
Of Jack and his brother,
And now my story is done.

176

DOCTOR FELL

I do not like thee, Doctor Fell,
The reason why I cannot tell;
But this I know, and know full well,
I do not like·thee, Doctor Fell.

FIRE

Fire! Fire! said Mrs Dyer;
Where? Where? said Mrs Dare;
Up the town, said Mrs Brown;
Any damage? said Mrs Gamage;
None at all, said Mrs Hall.

THE WIND

My lady Wind, my lady Wind,
Went round the house to find
  A chink to set her foot in;
She tried the key-hole in the door,
She tried the crevice in the floor,
  And drove the chimney soot in.

THE MULBERRY BUSH

Here we go round the mulberry bush,
The mulberry bush, the mulberry bush
Here we go round the mulberry bush,
On a cold and frosty morning.

This is the way we wash our hands,
Wash our hands, wash our hands,
This is the way we wash our hands,
On a cold and frosty morning.

This is the way we wash our clothes,
Wash our clothes, wash our clothes,
This is the way we wash our clothes,
On a cold and frosty morning.

This is the way we go to school,
Go to school, go to school,
This is the way we go to school,
On a cold and frosty morning.

This is the way we come out of school,
Come out of school, come out of school,
This is the way we come out of school,
On a cold and frosty morning.

WINTER

Cold and raw the north wind
    doth blow,
Bleak in the morning early;
All the hills are covered with
    snow,
And winter's now come fairly.

ONE MISTY, MOISTY MORNING

One misty, moisty morning,
  When cloudy was the weather,
I met a little old man
  Clothed all in leather.

He began to compliment,
  And I began to grin,
How do you do, and how do you do,
  And how do you do again?

THE BAD RIDER

I had a little pony,
  His name was Dapple Gray;
I lent him to a lady
  To ride a mile away.
She whipped him, she slashed him,
  She rode him through the mire;
I would not lend my pony now,
  For all the lady's hire.

MOLL-IN-THE-WAD
Moll-in-the-Wad and I fell out,
What do you think it was all about?
I gave her a shilling, she swore it
     was bad,
It's an old soldier's button, says
     Moll-in-the-Wad.

SIR SIMON THE KING
Old Sir Simon the king,
And young Sir Simon the squire,
And old Mrs Hickabout
Kicked Mrs Kickabout
Round about our coal fire.

OH THAT I WERE
Oh, that I were
    Where I would be,
Then would I be
    Where I am not;
But where I am
    There I must be,
And where I would be
    I can not.

BOYS AND GIRLS COME OUT TO PLAY

Boys and girls come out to play,
The moon doth shine as bright as day.
Leave your supper and leave your sleep,
And join your playfellows in the street.
Come with a whoop and come with a call,
Come with a good will or not at all.
Up the ladder and down the wall,
A half-penny loaf will serve us all;
You find milk, and I'll find flour,
And we'll have a pudding in half an hour.

DANCE TO YOUR DADDY

Dance to your daddy,
  My little babby,
Dance to your daddy,
  My little lamb.

You shall have a fishy
  In a little dishy,
You shall have a fishy
  When the boat comes in.

You shall have an apple,
  You shall have a plum,
You shall have a rattle-basket
  When your daddy comes home.

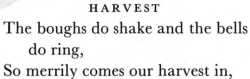

HARVEST

The boughs do shake and the bells
    do ring,
So merrily comes our harvest in,
Our harvest in, our harvest in,
So merrily comes our harvest in.

We've ploughed, we've sowed,
We've reaped, we've mowed,
We've got our harvest in.

BETTY BOTTER'S BATTER

Betty Botter bought some butter,
But, she said, the butter's bitter;
If I put it in my batter
It will make my batter bitter,
But a bit of better butter,
That would make my batter better.
So she bought a bit of butter
Better than her bitter butter,
And she put it in her batter
And the batter was not bitter.
So t'was better Betty Botter
Bought a bit of better butter.

JACK AND GYE

Jack and Gye
    Went out in the rye,
And they found a little boy
    With one black eye.
Come, says Jack,
    Let's knock him on the head.
No, says Gye,
    Let's buy him some bread;
You buy one loaf
    And I'll buy two,
And we'll bring him up
    As other folks do.

JENNY

Hie to the market, Jenny come trot,
Spilt all her butter milk, every drop,
Every drop and every dram,
Jenny came home with an empty can.

THREE ACRES OF LAND

My father left me three acres of land,
 Sing ivy, sing ivy;
My father left me three acres of land,
 Sing holly, go whistle and ivy!

I ploughed it with a ram's horn,
 Sing ivy, sing ivy;
And sowed it all over with one peppercorn,
 Sing holly, go whistle and ivy!

I harrowed it with a bramble bush,
 Sing ivy, sing ivy;
And reaped it with my little penknife,
 Sing holly, go whistle and ivy!

I got the mice to carry it to the barn,
 Sing ivy, sing ivy;
And thrashed it with a goose's quill,
 Sing holly, go whistle and ivy!

I got the cat to carry it to the mill,
 Sing ivy, sing ivy;
The miller he swore he would have her paw,
And the cat she swore she would scratch his face,
 Sing holly, go whistle and ivy!

PETER PIPER

Peter Piper picked a peck of pickled
 pepper;
A peck of pickled pepper Peter Piper
 picked.
If Peter Piper picked a peck of
 pickled pepper,
Where's the peck of pickled pepper
 Peter Piper picked?

CATCH HIM, CROW!

Catch him, crow! Carry him, kite!
Take him away till the apples are ripe;
When they are ripe and ready to fall,
Here comes baby, apples and all.

THE CROWS

On the first of March,
The crows begin to search;
By the first of April
They are sitting still;
By the first of May
They've all flown away,
Coming greedy back again
With October's wind and rain.

BANBURY FAIR

As I was going to Banbury,
    Upon a summer's day,
My dame had butter, eggs, and fruit,
    And I had corn and hay.
Joe drove the ox, and Tom the swine,
    Dick took the foal and mare;
I sold them all—then home to dine,
    From famous Banbury fair.

THE SOLDIER AND THE MAID

Oh, soldier, soldier, will you marry me,
    With your musket, fife, and drum?
Oh no, pretty maid, I cannot marry you,
    For I have no coat to put on.

Then away she went to the tailor's shop
    As fast as legs could run,
And bought him one of the very very best,
    And the soldier put it on.

Oh, soldier, soldier, will you marry me,
    With your musket, fife, and drum?
Oh no, pretty maid, I cannot marry you,
    For I have no shoes to put on.

Then away she went to the cobbler's shop
    As fast as legs could run,
And bought him a pair of the very very best,
    And the soldier put them on.

Oh, soldier, soldier, will you marry me,
    With your musket, fife, and drum?
Oh no, pretty maid, I cannot marry you,
    For I have no socks to put on.

Then away she went to the sock-maker's shop
    As fast as legs could run,
And bought him a pair of the very very best,
    And the soldier put them on.

Oh, soldier, soldier, will you marry me,
    With your musket, fife, and drum?
Oh no, pretty maid, I cannot marry you,
    For I have no hat to put on.

Then away she went to the hatter's shop
    As fast as legs could run,
And bought him one of the very very best,
    And the soldier put it on.

Oh, soldier, soldier, will you marry me,
    With your musket, fife, and drum?
Oh no, pretty maid, I cannot marry you,
    For I have a wife at home.

ALL WORK AND NO PLAY

All work and no play makes Jack a dull boy;
All play and no work makes Jack a mere toy.

THREE YOUNG RATS

Three young rats with black felt hats,
Three young ducks with white straw flats,
Three young dogs with curling tails,
Three young cats with demi-veils,
Went out to walk with three young pigs
In satin vests and sorrel wigs;
But suddenly it chanced to rain
And so they all went home again.

A LITTLE GIRL

When I was a little girl,
   About seven years old,
I hadn't got a petticoat,
   To keep me from the cold.

So I went into Darlington,
   That pretty little town,
And there I bought a petticoat,
   A cloak, and a gown.

I went into the woods
   And built me a kirk,
And all the birds of the air,
   They helped me to work.

The hawk, with his long claws,
   Pulled down the stone;
The dove with her rough bill,
   Brought me them home.

The parrot was the clergyman,
   The peacock was the clerk,
The bullfinch played the organ,
   And we made merry work.

MISTER RUSTICAP

As I went over Lincoln Bridge,
I met Mister Rusticap;
Pins and needles on his back,
A-going to Thorney fair.

UNCLE DAVY

As I went up a slippery gap
I met my Uncle Davy;
With timber toes and iron nose
Upon my word he would frighten the crows.

BLIND MAN'S BUFF

Blind man, blind man,
  Sure you can't see?
Turn round three times,
  And try to catch me.
Turn east, turn west,
  Catch as you can,
Did you think you'd caught me?
  Blind, blind man!

A WALNUT

As soft as silk, as white as milk,
As bitter as gall, a strong wall,
And a green coat covers me all.

THIS IS THE WAY THE LADIES RIDE

This is the way the ladies ride,
  Nim, nim, nim, nim.
This is the way the gentlemen ride,
  Trim, trim, trim, trim.
This is the way the farmers ride,
  Trot, trot, trot, trot.
This is the way the huntsmen ride,
  A-gallop, a-gallop, a-gallop, a-gallop.
This is the way the ploughboys ride,
  Hobble-dy-gee, hobble-dy-gee.

189

WHERE I WENT

I went up the high hill,
There I saw a climbing goat;
I went down by the running rill,
There I saw a ragged sheep;
I went out to the roaring sea,
There I saw a tossing boat;
I went under the green tree,
There I saw two doves asleep.

THE MILKMAID

Little maid, pretty maid,
  Whither goest thou?
Down in the forest
  To milk my cow.
Shall I go with thee?
  No, not now.
When I send for thee
  Then come thou.

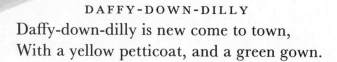

DAFFY-DOWN-DILLY

Daffy-down-dilly is new come to town,
With a yellow petticoat, and a green gown.

APPLES

Here's to thee, old apple tree,
Whence thou may'st bud
And whence thou may'st blow,
And whence thou may'st bear apples
    enow;
Hats full and caps full,
Bushels full and sacks full,
And our pockets full too.

THE HART

The hart he loves the high wood,
    The hare she loves the hill;
The knight he loves his bright sword,
    The lady loves her will.

THE WITCH'S SONG

I went to the toad that lies under the wall,
I charmed him out, and he came at my call;
I scratched out the eyes of the owl before,
I tore the bat's wing; what would you have more?

COUNTING RHYMES

One-ery, two-ery, tickery, seven,
Hallibo, crackibo, ten and eleven,
Spin, span, muskidan,
Twiddle-um, twaddle-um, twenty-
    one.

One-ery, two-ery, ickery, Ann,
Phillisy, phollisy, Nicholas John,
Quever, quaver, Irish Mary,
Stickerum, stackerum, buck.

TOBACCO

Make three-fourths of a cross,
  And a circle complete,
And let two semicircles
  On a perpendicular meet;
Next add a triangle
  That stands on two feet;
Next two semicircles
  And a circle complete.
      (Tobacco)

192

A TALE

There was an old woman sat spin-
    ning,
And that's the first beginning;
She had a calf,
And that's half;
She took it by the tail,
And threw it over the wall,
And that's all.

FISHES

Little fishes in a brook,
Father caught them on a hook,
Mother fried them in a pan,
Johnnie eats them like a man.

THE OLD WOMAN
AND THE MOUSE

There was an old woman
    Lived under a hill,
She put a mouse in a bag,
    And sent it to the mill.
The miller did swear
    By the point of his knife,
He never took toll
    Of a mouse in his life.

193

MISSING COMMAS

I saw a peacock with a fiery tail
I saw a blazing comet drop down hail
I saw a cloud with ivy curled around
I saw a sturdy oak creep on the ground
I saw an ant swallow up a whale
I saw a raging sea brim full of ale
I saw a Venice glass sixteen foot deep
I saw a well full of men's tears that weep
I saw their eyes all in a flame of fire
I saw a house high as the moon and higher
I saw the sun at twelve o'clock at night
I saw the man who saw this wondrous sight.

WIBBLETON AND WOBBLETON

From Wibbleton to Wobbleton is
    fifteen miles,
From Wobbleton to Wibbleton is
    fifteen miles,
From Wibbleton to Wobbleton,
From Wobbleton to Wibbleton,
From Wibbleton to Wobbleton is
    fifteen miles.

QUEEN CAROLINE

Queen, Queen Caroline,
Washed her hair in turpentine,
Turpentine to make it shine,
Queen, Queen Caroline.

TIT, TAT, TOE

Tit, tat, toe,
  My first go,
Three jolly butcher boys
    All in a row;
Stick one up, stick one down,
Stick one in the old man's crown.

THE LION AND THE UNICORN

The lion and the unicorn
　　Were fighting for the crown;
The lion beat the unicorn
　　All around the town.

Some gave them white bread,
　　And some gave them brown;
Some gave them plum cake
　　And drummed them out of town.

SEA SHELLS

She sells sea-shells on the sea shore;
The shells that she sells are sea-shells I'm sure.
So if she sells sea-shells on the sea shore,
I'm sure that the shells are sea-shore shells.

THE RUGGED ROCK

Round and round the rugged rock
The ragged rascal ran.
How many R's are there in that?
Now tell me if you can.

THE THREE JOVIAL WELSHMEI

There were three jovial Welshmen
    As I have heard men say,
And they would go a-hunting
    Upon St David's Day.

All the day they hunted
    And nothing could they find,
But a ship a-sailing,
    A-sailing with the wind.

One said it was a ship,
    The other he said, Nay;
The third said it was a house,
    With the chimney blown away.

And all the night they hunted
    And nothing could they find,
But the moon a-gliding,
    A-gliding with the wind.

One said it was the moon,
    The other he said, Nay;
The third said it was a cheese,
    And half of it cut away.

And all the day they hunted
  And nothing could they find,
But a hedgehog in a bramble bush,
  And that they left behind.

The first said it was a hedgehog,
  The second he said, Nay;
The third said it was a pincushion,
  And the pins stuck in wrong way.

And all the night they hunted
  And nothing could they find,
But a hare in a turnip field,
  And that they left behind.

The first said it was a hare,
  The second he said, Nay;
The third said it was a calf,
  And the cow had run away.

And all the day they hunted
  And nothing could they find,
But an owl in a holly tree,
  And that they left behind.

One said it was an owl,
  The other he said, Nay;
The third said 'twas an old man,
  And his beard growing grey.

WHAT CAN THE MATTER BE?

O dear, what can the matter be?
Dear, dear, what can the matter be?
O dear, what can the matter be?
Johnny's so long at the fair.

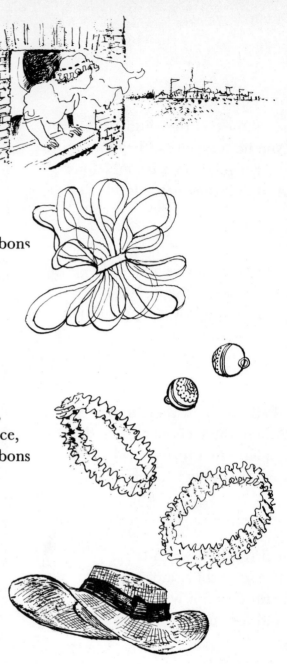

He promised he'd buy me a fairing
   should please me,
And then for a kiss, oh! he vowed
   he would tease me,
He promised he'd bring me a bunch of blue ribbons
To tie up my bonny brown hair.

And it's O dear, what can the matter be?
Dear, dear, what can the matter be?
O dear, what can the matter be?
Johnny's so long at the fair.

He promised to buy me a pair of sleeve buttons,
A pair of new garters that cost him but two pence,
He promised he'd bring me a bunch of blue ribbons
To tie up my bonny brown hair.

And it's O dear, what can the matter be?
Dear, dear, what can the matter be?
O dear, what can the matter be?
Johnny's so long at the fair.

He promised he'd bring me a basket of posies,
A garland of lilies, a garland of roses,
A little straw hat, to set off the blue ribbons
That tie up my bonny brown hair.

THE LITTLE GIRL

There was a little girl, and she had a little curl
   Right in the middle of her forehead;
When she was good she was very, very good,
   But when she was bad she was horrid.

SWINGING

I went into my grandmother's
  garden
And there I found a farden,
I gave it to my mother
To buy a baby brother;
The baby was so bandy,
I gave it a drop of brandy;
The brandy was so hot,
I put it in the pot;
The pot was so little,
I put it in the kettle;
The kettle had a spout
And it all ran out.
    With a good push –
    Over the bowling green.

THE FEATURES

Eye winker,
Tom Tinker,
Nose smeller,
Mouth eater,
Chin chopper,
Guzzlewopper.

DUSTY MILLER

O the little rusty dusty miller,
Dusty was his coat,
Dusty was his colour,
Dusty was the kiss
I got from the miller.
If I had my pockets
Full of gold and siller,
I would give it all
To my dusty miller.

MOSES

Moses supposes his toeses are roses,
But Moses supposes erroneously;
For nobody's toeses are posies of
    roses
As Moses supposes his toeses to be.

A PRETTY WENCH

I am a pretty wench,
    And I come a great way hence,
And sweethearts I can get none:
    But every dirty sow
    Can get sweethearts enough,
And I pretty wench can get none.

ALLIGOSHEE

Darby and Joan were dressed in
  black,
Sword and buckle behind their back;
Foot for foot, and knee for knee,
Turn about Darby's company.

GUNPOWDER PLOT DAY

Please to remember
The Fifth of November,
Gunpowder treason and plot;
I see no reason
Why gunpowder treason
Should ever be forgot.

203

THE MILK MAID

Where are you going to, my pretty maid?
I'm going a-milking, sir, she said,
Sir, she said, sir, she said,
I'm going a-milking, sir, she said.

May I go with you, my pretty maid?
You're kindly welcome, sir, she said,
Sir, she said, sir, she said,
You're kindly welcome, sir, she said.

Say, will you marry me, my pretty maid?
Yes, if you please, kind sir, she said,
Sir, she said, sir, she said,
Yes, if you please, kind sir, she said.

What is your father, my pretty maid?
My father's a farmer, sir, she said,
Sir, she said, sir, she said,
My father's a farmer, sir, she said.

What is your fortune, my pretty maid?
My face is my fortune, sir, she said,
Sir, she said, sir, she said,
My face is my fortune, sir, she said.

Then I can't marry you, my pretty maid.
Nobody asked you, sir, she said,
Sir, she said, sir, she said,
Nobody asked you, sir, she said.

THE OLD WOMAN

Old woman, old woman,
   Shall we go a-shearing?
Speak a little louder, sir,
   I'm very thick of hearing.
Old woman, old woman,
   Shall I love you dearly?
Thank you very kindly, sir,
   Now I hear you clearly.

A SAD SONG

Trip upon trenchers, and dance upon dishes,
My mother sent me for some barm, some barm;
She bid me tread lightly, and come again quickly,
For fear the young men should do me some harm.
   Yet didn't you see, yet didn't you see,
   What naughty tricks they put upon me:
     They broke my pitcher,
     And spilt the water,
     And huffed my mother,
     And chid her daughter,
And kissed my sister instead of me.

BAGPIPES

Puss came dancing out of a barn
With a pair of bagpipes under her arm;
She could sing nothing but, Fiddle cum fee,
The mouse has married the humble-bee.
Pipe, cat – dance, mouse –
We'll have a wedding at our good house.

A fox jumped up one winter's night,
And begged the moon to give him light,
For he'd many miles to trot that night
Before he reached his den O!
    Den O! Den O!
For he'd many miles to trot that night
Before he reached his den O!

The first place he came to was a farmer's yard,
Where the ducks and the geese declared it hard
That their nerves should be shaken and their rest so marred
By a visit from Mr Fox O!
    Fox O! Fox O!
That their nerves should be shaken and their rest so marred
By a visit from Mr Fox O!

He took the grey goose by the neck,
And swung him right across his back;
The grey goose cried out, Quack, quack, quack,
With his legs hanging dangling down O!
    Down O! Down O!
The grey goose cried out, Quack, quack, quack,
With his legs hanging dangling down O!

Old Mother Slipper Slopper jumped out of bed,
And out of the window she popped her head:
Oh! John, John, John, the grey goose is gone,
And the fox is off to his den O!
    Den O! Den O!
Oh! John, John, John, the grey goose is gone,
And the fox is off to his den O!

John ran up to the top of the hill,
And blew his whistle loud and shrill;
Said the fox, That is very pretty music; still—
I'd rather be in my den O!
    Den O! Den O!
Said the fox, That is very pretty music; still—
I'd rather be in my den O!

The fox went back to his hungry den,
And his dear little foxes, eight, nine, ten;
Quoth they, Good daddy, you must go there again,
If you bring such good cheer from the farm O!
     Farm O! Farm O!
Quoth they, Good daddy, you must go there again,
If you bring such good cheer from the farm O!

The fox and his wife, without any strife,
Said they never ate a better goose in all their life:
They did very well without fork or knife,
And the little ones picked the bones O!
     Bones O! Bones O!
They did very well without fork or knife,
And the little ones picked the bones O!

BEDTIME

The Man in the Moon looked
     out of the moon,
   Looked out of the moon
     and said,
" 'Tis time for all children
     on the earth
   To think about getting to bed!"

THE MOON

I see the moon,
   And the moon sees me;
God bless the moon,
   And God bless me.

THE OWL

Of all the gay birds that e'er I did see,
The owl is the fairest by far to me,
For all day long she sits in a tree,
And when the night comes away flies she.

THE WEDDING

This year,
Next year,
Sometime,
Never.

Coach,
Carriage,
Wheelbarrow,
Dustcart.

Gold,
Silver,
Copper,
Brass.

Silk,	Big box,	Boots,	Church,	Big house,
Satin,	Little box,	Shoes,	Chapel,	Little house
Cotton,	Band box,	Slippers,	Cathedral,	Pig sty,
Rags.	Bundle.	Clogs.	Abbey.	Barn.

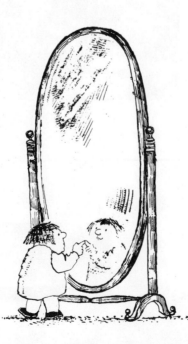

BY MYSELF

As I walked by myself
And talked to myself,
  Myself said unto me,
Look to thyself,
Take care of thyself,
  For nobody cares for thee.

I answered myself,
And said to myself
  In the self-same repartee,
Look to thyself,
Or not to thyself,
  The self-same thing will be.

WINE AND CAKES

Wine and cakes for gentlemen,
Hay and corn for horses,
A cup of ale for good old wives,
And kisses for young lasses.

THE GIRL IN THE LANE

The girl in the lane,
That couldn't speak plain,
    Cried, Gobble, gobble, gobble.
The man on the hill,
That couldn't stand still,
    Went hobble, hobble, hobble.

THREE GHOSTESSES

Three little ghostesses,
Sitting on postesses,
Eating buttered toastesses,
Greasing their fistesses,
Up to their wristesses.
Oh, what beastesses
To make such feastesses!

209

NOTHING-AT-ALL

There was an old woman called Nothing-
at-all,
Who lived in a dwelling exceedingly
small;
A man stretched his mouth to its utmost
extent,
And down at one gulp house and old
woman went.

SQUABBLES

My little old man and I fell out,
How shall we bring this matter
about?
Bring it about as well as you can,
And get you gone, you little old
man!

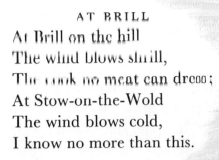

AT BRILL

At Brill on the hill
The wind blows shrill,
The cook no meat can dress;
At Stow-on-the-Wold
The wind blows cold,
I know no more than this.

SING JIGMIJOLE

Sing jigmijole, the pudding bowl,
    The table and the frame;
My master he did cudgel me,
    For kissing of my dame.

THE THREE LITTLE KITTENS

Three little kittens
They lost their mittens,
   And they began to cry,
Oh, Mother dear,
We sadly fear
   Our mittens we have lost.
What! lost your mittens,
You naughty kittens!
   Then you shall have no pie.
   Mee-ow, mee-ow, mee-ow.
   No, you shall have no pie.

The three little kittens
Put on their mittens
And soon ate up the pie;
Oh, Mother dear,
We greatly fear
   Our mittens we have soiled.
What! soiled your mittens,
You naughty kittens!
   Then they began to sigh,
Mee-ow, mee-ow, mee-ow,
Then they began to sigh.

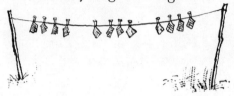

The three little kittens
They found their mittens,
   And they began to cry,
Oh, Mother dear,
See here, see here,
   Our mittens we have found.
Put on your mittens,
You silly kittens,
   And you shall have some pie.
   Purr-r, purr-r, purr-r,
   Oh, let us have some pie.

The three little kittens
They washed their mittens,
   And hung them out to dry;
Oh, Mother dear,
Do you not hear,
   Our mittens we have washed.
What! washed your mittens,
Then you're good kittens,
   But I smell a rat close by.
   Mee-ow, mee-ow,
      mee-ow,
We smell a rat
   close by.

BUFF

I had a dog
Whose name was Buff;
I sent him for
   A bag of snuff;
He broke the bag
   And spilt the stuff,
And that was all
   My penny's worth.

RIDE AWAY

Ride away, ride away,
　Johnny shall ride,
He shall have a pussy cat
　Tied to one side;
He shall have a little dog
　Tied to the other,
And Johnny shall ride
　To see his grandmother.

TWO MILLS

My mill grinds pepper and spice;
Your mill grinds rats and mice.

THE DONKEY

Donkey, donkey, old and gray,
Ope your mouth and gently bray;
Lift your ears and blow your horn,
To wake the world this sleepy morn.

OLD FARMER GILES

Old Farmer Giles,
　He went seven miles
With his faithful dog Old Rover;
　And Old Farmer Giles,
　When he came to the stiles,
Took a run, and jumped clean over.

TOM THUMB'S PICTURE ALPHABET
A was an archer,
      who shot at a frog;
B was a butcher,
      and had a great dog.
C was a captain,
      all covered with lace;
D was a drunkard,
      and had a red face.
E was an esquire,
      with pride on his brow;
F was a farmer,
      and followed the plough.
G was a gamester,
      who had but ill-luck;
H was a hunter,
      and hunted a buck.
I was an innkeeper,
      who loved to carouse;
J was a joiner,
      and built up a house.
K was King William,
      once governed this land;
L was a lady,
      who had a white hand.
M was a miser,
      and hoarded up gold;

N was a nobleman,
>> gallant and bold.
O was an oyster girl,
>> and went about town;
P was a parson,
>> and wore a black gown.
Q was a queen,
>> who wore a silk slip;
R was a robber,
>> and wanted a whip.
S was a sailor,
>> and spent all he got;
T was a tinker,
>> and mended a pot.
U was a userer,
>> a miserable elf;
V was a vintner,
>> who drank all himself.
W was a watchman,
>> and guarded the door;
X was expensive,
>> and so became poor.
Y was a youth,
>> that did not love school;
Z was a zany,
>> a poor harmless fool.

THE LITTLE MAN AND THE LITTLE MAID

There was a little man,
And he wooed a little maid,
And he said, Little maid, will you wed, wed, wed?
I have little more to say,
Than will you, yea or nay?
For the least said is soonest mended, ded, ded.

Then this little maid she said,
Little sir, you've little said,
To induce a little maid for to wed, wed, wed;
You must say a little more,
And produce a little ore,
Ere I to the church will be led, led, led.

Then the little man replied,
If you'll be my little bride,
I will raise my love notes a little higher, higher, higher;
Though I little love to prate
You will find my heart is great,
With the little God of Love all on fire, fire, fire.

Then the little maid replied,
If I should be your bride,
Pray, what must we have for to eat, eat, eat?
Will the flames that you're so rich in
Make a fire in the kitchen,
And the little God of Love turn the spit, spit, spit?

Then the little man he sighed,
And some say a little cried,
And his little heart was big with sorrow, sorrow, sorrow;
I'll be your little slave,
And if the little that I have,
Be too little, little dear, I will borrow, borrow, borrow.

Then the little man so gent,
Made the little maid relent,
And set her little soul a-thinking, king, king;
Though his little was but small,
Yet she had his little all,
And could have of a cat but her skin, skin, skin.

SCOTTISH LULLABY

Hush-a-ba birdie, croon, croon,
Hush-a-ba birdie, croon,
The sheep are gane to the silver wood,
And the cows are gane to the broom, broom.

And it's braw milking the kye, kye,
It's braw milking the kye,
The birds are singing, the bells are ringing,
The wild deer come galloping by, by.

And hush-a-ba birdie, croon, croon,
Hush-a-ba birdie, croon,
The gaits are gane to the mountain hie,
And they'll no be hame till noon, noon.

Encore till the child's asleep

217

Index to first lines and titles